D1431998

Buying Styles

*Simple Lessons in
Selling the Way Your Customer Buys*

MICHAEL WILKINSON

WITH RICHARD SMITH, TIERAH CHORBA, AND LYNN SOKLER

BAKER COLLEGE OF
CLINTON TWP. LIBRARY

 American Management
Association®

AMERICAN MANAGEMENT ASSOCIATION

New York • Atlanta • Brussels • Chicago • Mexico City • San Francisco
Shanghai • Tokyo • Toronto • Washington, D.C.

Special discounts on bulk quantities of AMACOM books are available to corporations, professional associations, and other organizations. For details, contact Special Sales Department, AMACOM, a division of American Management Association, 1601 Broadway, New York, NY 10019.
Tel: 212-903-8316. Fax: 212-903-8083.
E-mail: specialsls@amanet.org
Website: www.amacombooks.org/go/specialsales
To view all AMACOM titles go to: www.amacombooks.org

This publication is designed to provide accurate and authoritative information in regard to the subject matter covered. It is sold with the understanding that the publisher is not engaged in rendering legal, accounting, or other professional service. If legal advice or other expert assistance is required, the services of a competent professional person should be sought.

Library of Congress Cataloging-in-Publication Data

Wilkinson, Michael, 1957-
  Buying styles : simple lessons in selling the way your customer buys / Michael Wilkinson ; with Richard Smith, Tierah Chorba, and Lynn Sokler.
    p. cm.
  Includes bibliographical references and index.
  ISBN-13: 978-0-8144-1527-6
  ISBN-10: 0-8144-1527-X
  1. Selling. 2. Consumers' preferences. 3. Consumer satisfaction. I. Title.

HF5438.25.W2983 2009
658.85—dc22
                                                                    2009003706

© 2009 Michael Wilkinson.
All rights reserved.
Printed in the United States of America.

This publication may not be reproduced, stored in a retrieval system, or transmitted in whole or in part, in any form or by any means, electronic, mechanical, photocopying, recording, or otherwise, without the prior written permission of AMACOM, a division of American Management Association, 1601 Broadway, New York, NY 10019.

Printing number
10 9 8 7 6 5 4 3 2 1

• • • • • • • • • • • •

To Lelita, Linda, Randy, Terry, Michele, Mom, and Dad—my earliest teachers in selling the way your customer buys.

• • • • • • • • • • • •

Contents

Acknowledgments

No book is written without the support of many. As the principal author, I first want to thank my coauthors, whose unique contributions have made *Buying Styles* a much better book.

- Thank you, Lynn, for driving the creation of the training class on which this book is based.

- Tierah, thanks for the work you put into creating the case studies and brainstorming approaches to incorporating reviewer suggestions.

- And thanks, Richard, for your wisdom in guiding the choices we made and for your continued commitment to high excellence in all that we do.

Thanks to the team at Leadership Strategies—The Facilitation Company, without whose support this book would still be just another good idea.

I also want to thank the many people who reviewed the work and made suggestions along the way, especially Chris Valley, Jim Hamilton, Todd Hutto, Victor Kubik, Rick Kennamer, Jeff Hall, Tony Mazza, Lyman Jordan, and Bri Pennie.

Special thanks to Adam Shapiro (Mr. CustomerCentric Selling in the southeast), whose unique perspective and insights challenged our thinking and helped drive us to a better result.

Thanks to Jessie Block at Target Training International for her help with the book and to Art Shoeck at Data Dome for introducing me to the DISC styles survey more than 15 years ago.

Thanks to my Vistage chair, Larry Hart, and my fellow Vistage members in 603, who continue to hold me accountable for working *on* the company and not *in* the company.

Thanks to the team at AMACOM and especially my editor, Bob Nirkind, who saw the vision and the power of the learning adventure when so many others couldn't.

Finally, to my family, Sherry, Danielle, and Gabrielle. The love and the awesome support I feel from you help me excel at doing what I have been called to do. Simply, thanks.

Michael Wilkinson

November 2008

Introduction

What This Book Will Do for You

"I hate it when salespeople _____"

Fill in the blank. Think about some of your worse experiences with salespeople. Think about the things that salespeople have done that turned you off. How would you fill in the blank? Do you hate it when . . .

- They are pushy?
- They don't get to the point?
- They don't know their product?
- They bore you with facts and figures?
- They don't listen or take the time to understand you and your needs?

Now for the more important question: How would *your customers* fill in the blank? If your answer is, "It depends on the customer," then you are ready for this book.

Our purpose with *Buying Styles: Simple Lessons for Selling the Way Your Customer Buys* is to provide an entertaining quick read that helps sales professionals learn the primary buying styles of customers, as well as how to identify and adapt to each. Unfortunately, many salespeople know only one way to sell—*their way*. What they often fail to understand is that they could be so much more successful by selling the way their customer buys.

Do you sell the same way to every customer? Do you know the basic buying styles and the key strategies for adapting to each one? Do you know the warning signs that suggest you are probably selling in the wrong style for your customer?

The message of *Buying Styles* is simple. As our protagonist says:

> **"Adapt or continue to be so much less successful than you could be."**

With *Buying Styles*, we introduce a powerful new book format called the "learning adventure." Somewhat similar to a parable, this learning adventure tells the story of a fictional character, Dave, who has just lost a major sale and is clueless as to why. At the urging of his CEO, Dave attends a half-day seminar on buying styles.

Unlike in a parable, however, the meat of the book is not buried at the end of the story. In our learning adventure,

90 percent of the story takes place in the classroom. Therefore, the story *is* the meat.

This learning adventure provides a powerful vehicle for readers to gain insights in three ways:

- You *receive* the buying styles concepts directly from the story's course facilitator as if you were sitting in the classroom along with Dave.

- At the same time, you *experience* the information through Dave's eyes. You hear his objections, his concerns, and his fears, and you feel his triumphs as he gains insight as to why he lost this major sale while other sales had been so much easier for him.

- While in the learning adventure, you *observe* the interactions of the various people in the classroom and are able to recognize the buying style and selling style conflicts as they play out on a personal level.

Since our intended audience is salespeople, we have designed *Buying Styles* to be a series of short chapters, with each one contributing significantly to the message of the book. However, for those readers who want to cut to the chase (and you'll learn in Chapter 3 why you feel this way), we suggest you first read Chapters 3, 5, and 7.

- Chapter 3 provides you with a foundational understanding of the four basic buying styles.

- Chapter 5 presents you with the techniques for identifying the buying style of your customer.

- Chapter 7 offers you a summary for how to sell to each style.

Once you have read these targeted sections, you may want to go back and pick up the information in the other chapters to more fully understand the concept of buying styles.

For all other readers who wish to get the comprehensive message the first time, grab your highlighter and get ready for an adventure in learning to sell the way your customer buys.

....

CHAPTER 1

Looking for Solutions

....

*"Have you considered that we may have been selling
to her the wrong way?"*

....

Silence followed the question from the CEO of CRM First. The CEO was meeting with Dave, the company's sales director, and the sales representative, after they had lost a half-million-dollar contract to an inferior competitor. The potential client, Web Systems and Tools, one of the top Web site developers in the country, had agreed that CRM First had the better product, with richer features. And, though the product was slightly more expensive than the competitor's, the client's buyer had assured CRM First that its product's price was well within the budget that had been established.

The buyer, Sharlene Case, was cordial when she called with the bad news. "Your team did an admirable job," she stated. "You have a very good product—perhaps the most robust features among the ones we looked at. But, overall, we felt more comfortable working with the other team."

When Dave probed further by asking what his team could have done better, Sharlene stood her ground. "There was really nothing you could have done," she said. "You know how sometimes you click better with some people. We just had a lot more confidence in the other team's ability to follow through and meet our needs."

When he saw the opening, the sales rep desperately grabbed it. "Follow through? If you have a question about our ability to follow through, I can assure you that our operations team is awesome with follow-through."

In an effort to mask her irritation, Sharlene simply replied, "You may very well be able to back up your claim, but we have made our decision. However, if we have any additional needs in the future, I will not hesitate to ask your team to submit a bid. Thanks again for your effort."

And, with that, the phone call ended.

During the debriefing, Dave struggled to determine what he and his team had done wrong. From their sales process training, he believed they had done this one by the book:

- They had initiated the contact and generated the interest in implementing a client relationship management solution.

- They had worked with the client to define the need and to quantify the value.

- They had worked with the team to build an implementation plan.

- They had identified the various buyers, recommenders, and influencers and had executed plans to manage each.

- They had put together a champion letter— an e-mail after the first meeting that documented the client's need and the benefits to solving the need—and the client had made only slight modifications to the letter.

- They had gotten the client to agree to a specific sequence of events that would lead up to the sale and a qualifying event that would serve to verify the capabilities of the CRM First product.

- And, when the buyer asked for two additional bids, they had worked with the buyer's project manager to identify two known competitors, one lower priced and one higher priced, who would be eclipsed by the moderately priced, feature-rich solution that the CRM First product offered.

So why did they lose? The CEO's question loomed large.

> "Have you considered that we may have
> been selling to her the wrong way?"

"What do you mean?" Dave asked after a long silence. "We sold to her using the same strategies that have worked for us a hundred times. We identified the key influencers. We built the relationships. We must have wined and dined people in that organization a dozen times. We helped the buyer define the need. We had tech support provide a high-level cost-benefit analysis. We delivered a bullet-point, four-color proposal that was brief and to the point. So why do you think we sold to her the wrong way?"

"I really don't know," the CEO confessed. "I just have this nagging suspicion that we are missing something important here. We do win our share of the big ones. But my sense is that there may be something very different about the times when we win and the times when we lose."

"Yeah, when we lose, I don't get paid," quipped the sales rep.

"Dave," the CEO continued, "one of the other CEOs in my accountability group e-mailed a notice about a seminar he attended on something called buying styles. He was pretty high on it. Before our last group meeting, I took a quick look at the notice so that, if he asked, I could at least say I had glanced at it. However, the tagline caught my attention and has stuck with me: 'Simple lessons for selling the way your customer buys.' Could it be that we are selling to some of our potential clients the wrong way? I don't know. But it may be well worth the investment to find out. It looks like there is a session coming up in a few weeks. I'll forward you the information. Why don't you attend and see if it is something we can use?"

··

Could it be that we are selling to some of our potential clients the wrong way?

··

Dave was far from intrigued. "Buying styles?" he asked. "That sounds like some textbook mumbo jumbo taught by academics who wouldn't know a sales opportunity if it bit them. I have no desire to sit through a week of boring lectures."

"Look, it's only half a day, and the other CEO said the course was interactive and focused on real-world examples. Go ahead and look over the material, and, if it is not a session you can make, let's have someone else on your team attend. Does that work for you?"

CHAPTER 2

Identifying the Behaviors We Hate from Customers

"Think about the types of customers with whom you find it difficult to communicate. Think about their behaviors—the things they say and do that drive you nuts, the behaviors that just burn you. Now, in your teams, build a list of those customer communication behaviors that you hate."

Interesting way to start, Dave thought. Having been a veteran of numerous sales seminars, he had very low expectations for the four-hour session. Most sessions like this would have a "talking head" preaching to a room of a couple of hundred people.

The first sign that this might be a different experience was that the confirmation notice emphasized the importance of his coming to the class with a completed questionnaire about three customers recently acquired, three prospects that had been lost to a competitor, and three active prospects he was trying to sell. The second sign was that, when he entered the room, there were only four tables, with seating for 20, rather than rows of chairs for 200.

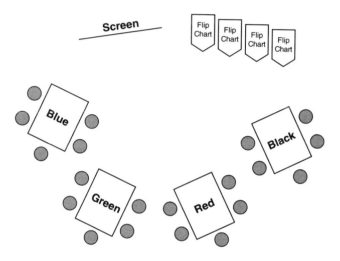

Dave's name card had a dot that indicated he would be a member of the "Red Team." He looked at the name cards that made up the rest of the Red Team:

The Red Team

- Connie—chief executive, Cassidy Accountants
- Ian—sales manager, US Classic Cars
- Dave—sales manager, CRM First
- Douglas—branch manager, United Bank and Trust
- Sam—sales representative, Premiere Telecom

And now, within the first five minutes of beginning, the facilitator was asking the participants to work in teams to identify the communication behaviors they found most difficult. His five-member team went straight to work. Douglas, the branch manager from the local bank, grabbed a pen first and asked, "Okay, who's got something?" Ian, the sales manager from the auto dealership, offered, "I hate it when customers waste your time gathering all this information about different cars for them, but then they end up doing nothing."

"All right, I got that one. What else?" Douglas asked. Dave added his thought: "I hate it when the real buyer refuses to speak with us and sends us back to the purchasing department. Because of the nature of our products, we need to build strong relationships with the people with whom we are going to work. The purchasing department just gets in the way of people talking."

Connie, the head of a small accounting firm, offered her view: "I hate it when customers aren't clear exactly what they want or when they end up changing things at the last minute."

Douglas turned to the last person at the table and asked, "What about you?" Sam, the sales rep from the telecommunications company, commented, "Well, I know my prospects are busy, but it is a bit irritating when you spend time with them initially, and then they don't bother to return your phone calls."

Douglas added his view: "And I hate it when customers want to tell you their whole life story. It never has anything to do with what they want to buy from me."

When the activity was finished, the Red Team's list included the following:

Behaviors We Hate from Customers

- They waste your time and then do nothing.
- The buyer sends you to purchasing.
- They aren't clear what they want, and they change things.
- They don't return your phone calls.
- They want to tell you their life story.

After the teams reviewed their lists with the rest of the class, the facilitator took over.

"When we are done this morning," he said, "you will understand that you have just told me more about yourselves then you have about your customers. As you will see, the behaviors you hate from your customers are usually just the opposite of your own selling style. And when your customer's buying style differs from your natural selling style, the result can be disastrous. Let me give you an example.

"My wife and I are busy people and don't have a lot of time to waste. Yet we think of ourselves as educated buyers. We want the information we need, when we need it, and in the form we need it so that we can quickly make a decision. When a personal friend approached us about purchasing life insurance many years back, we were ready for a quick education so that we could move to a decision. My friend, however, didn't get it. During the first two-hour meeting in our home, he took us through a laborious, detailed questionnaire to document our needs. My wife dropped out and went off and did something else while I completed the questionnaire. But then my friend wanted to schedule a second meeting to present options after analyzing the information. My wife and I both would have preferred that he had sent us the questionnaire ahead of time to eliminate the need for the second meeting, but we went along and scheduled the meeting that our friend had requested.

"When my friend returned, we knew we were in trouble within the first five minutes," the facilitator continued. "He insisted on taking us through a 40-slide canned presentation. Each time we tried to get him to skip through it quickly, he insisted that we needed to see every slide. It was painful, but we went along with it because he was a friend.

"It was the last straw, though, when we asked him specific questions about why he was suggesting a product and his repeated response was, 'For your situation, this is the best product for you. You have to trust me on this.' He didn't get it. He wanted to earn our trust by spending time with us. What he didn't understand was that trust for us was based on his being respectful of our time and answering our questions. Though we had been presold, he lost our business because he insisted on selling to us in his style, which had been successful for him with other customers, rather than in our buying style.

"How much business have you or your team lost simply because you weren't selling the way your customer buys?" the facilitator asked. "How much more business do you think you could win if you understood the four basic buying styles? That's what we are going to cover next: What are those buying styles? How do you recognize them? And how do you adapt to them?"

··

Though we had been presold,
he lost our business because he insisted on
selling to us in his style.

··

CHAPTER 3

Recognizing the Four Basic Buying Styles

. . . .

"Have you considered that we may have been selling to her the wrong way?"

. . . .

D ave's mind was buzzing. The CEO's question came back to him again. Could it be that his company had lost the half-million-dollar business with Web Systems and Tools principally because he and his team were selling in the wrong style? He looked down at the list of nine customers and prospects he had brought with him. He focused on the three losses: Web Systems and Tools, Global Tech Electronics, and The Candy Company. Was one of the losses, or possibly all three, a result of his team not understanding buying styles? Dave was ready to learn more.

The facilitator continued by explaining that the information on buying styles he was going to share was based on a research study of 15,000 people by Dr. William Marston in 1928. The study focused on communication styles and had been adapted for use in describing buying styles.

"There are four basic buying styles, which are indicated by the initials D-I-S-C. Each of us uses all four styles in our communication, but to varying degrees. And, at any given time in a sales transaction, one of these styles dominates your buyer's communication. Let's go through each of the four styles, starting with the high-D."

The High-D Style
● ●

"In the DISC model, D stands for drive or dominance. Imagine that there is a wall in front of us, and the objective is to get to the other side of the wall. High-Ds lower their shoulders, get a running start, and break through the wall. High-Ds get things done. They take a direct, assertive approach to solving problems. They enjoy challenges and get satisfaction from overcoming them. While the rest of us wake up and wonder what day it is, high-Ds wake up and immediately begin thinking about what they are going to get done that day.

"When you think of high-Ds, think of entrepreneurs, team leaders, and directors. What's the value to the organization of high-Ds? You probably have already figured it out. High-Ds focus their efforts on getting the job done, they address problems directly, and they make tough decisions quickly. Unfortunately, they also have a down side."

"Don't I know it," Dave said under his breath. High-Ds were not the type with whom he preferred to work. Although they knew what they wanted and didn't take a lot of time making a decision, they were often abrasive and had little interest in taking time to build relationships. When he would try to arrange meetings, he would be pushed down to underlings.

The facilitator continued, "You know when you are in the presence of high-Ds. They are always pushing. They always want to win—no matter the cost. They also tend to be so concerned about the goal that they don't consider the impact on people. And they tend to make decisions too quickly before having all the facts.

"Why do they do this? Because of their *key factor—time*. When you think of high-Ds, think 'time.' Don't waste their time. They have too much to do. So how do you sell to a high-D? Well, think of it this way."

The facilitator put up the following chart:

High-D Key Factor: Time

Selling Do's	Selling Don'ts
1. Be prepared; tell them what you are going to tell them.	1. Don't waste their time with idle chatter.
2. State your points clearly, *briefly*, specifically.	2. Don't ramble or tell long stories.
3. Give only as much detail as necessary; let them control.	3. Don't be too detailed unless they ask for it.

After reviewing the information in the table, the facilitator concluded, "To summarize, you can remember how to sell to this group by keeping in mind this key phrase for high-Ds:

High-D: Be prepared, be brief, be gone.

"Before we move on to the next style," the facilitator said, "look over your list of customers and principal buyers. Do you think any of these buyers are high-Ds? What are the signs that tell you this? Go ahead and complete the last two columns for the high-D accounts on your list."

Dave was sure that he had on occasion won with high-Ds, but the only high-Ds he recognized on his list were The Candy Company, a loss, and Regent Imaging Corporation, an account he was currently trying to sell. Dave completed the last two columns on his page for these two accounts.

Client	Key Buyer	Status	Style	The Signs
Fasteners in a Snap	Jillian McFarland, Vice President of Administration	Win		
Better Beverage Makers	Bob Scott, Chief Executive Officer	Win		
Ebank Finances	Vance Paulson, Director of European Expansion Unit	Win		
Web Systems and Tools	Sharlene Case, Vice President of Administration and Technology	Loss		

Client	Key Buyer	Status	Style	The Signs
Global Tech Electronic Specialists	Myron Griffin, Senior Vice President	Loss		
The Candy Company	Fiona Young, Vice President of Sales	Loss	D	• Wanted someone to "just get it done" • Had no interest in depth and breadth of features • Had unrealistic expectations on delivery time
Financial Compliance Advisers	Geoffrey Wilson, Chief Executive Officer	Active		
Regent Imaging Corporation	Ross Studebaker, Chief Operating Officer	Active	D	• All meetings short and to the point • Pushed us down to work with lower people in his organization • When named head of the project midway through, did not review any of the previous documentation
Premier Granite and Tile	John Eric, Vice President of Operations	Active		

The High-I Style

• •

After doing a quick review of the high-D style, the facilitator continued. "We talked about the high-D. Let's move on to the second major style in the DISC model. *I* stands for influence. High-Is enjoy helping people see the big picture. They motivate and inspire others to succeed. While high-Ds break through the wall, high-Is motivate people over the wall. They are the ones with the megaphone yelling, 'Hey, everyone. We have a wall to get over. Come on. It will be great on the other side. We can do it. Go, team! Go, team! Over the wall!'

"When you think of high-Is, think of salespeople, teachers, and facilitators. What's the value to the organization of high-Is? High-Is are able to see the big picture. They are great at motivating and selling others. They create a dynamic environment that is almost always fun. They like relationships and working with people. They are also highly creative. I'm sure you have all heard the term 'Think outside the box.' High-Is don't even see the box. They are the ones who are naturally creative and come up with innovative solutions."

Dave knew right away that this was the group to whom he liked selling the most. Though he didn't always win, it was always comfortable, and he had a good time dealing with them. These people knew that the key to long-term success was relationships. They wanted to deal with people they liked and didn't mind taking the time to talk.

Dave was brought out of his daydream when he heard the facilitator add, "But, like the high-Ds, high-Is also have a downside. They can be so talkative that they don't listen. They can also spend so much time on the vision that they never execute or buy anything. And, because they focus on ideas, they tend to overlook details.

"Why do they do this? Because of their *key factor: being heard.* High-Is like the stage. They enjoy having an audience with whom to interact.

"So how do you sell to a high-I? Take a look at the following chart."

High-I Key Factor: Being Heard

Selling Do's	Selling Don'ts
1. Give them the big picture before going into details.	1. Don't dwell on details and facts; provide them in writing, instead.
2. Give them a chance to share their ideas.	2. Don't tell them what to do without giving them an opportunity to respond.
3. Keep the conversation friendly and warm.	3. Don't allow them to ramble too long.

"To summarize," the facilitator concluded, "you can remember how to sell to this group by keeping in mind this key phrase for high-Is:

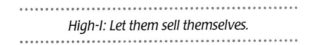

High-I: Let them sell themselves.

"See, if *you* are trying to sell to a high-I, the wrong person is speaking! If you want to sell high-Is, you have to get *them* talking about *your* solution. Ask them what they need in a solution. Ask them to describe how it would work. Then, after outlining your solution, ask them to talk about the benefits. Remember, you have to let them sell themselves.

"As before," said the facilitator, "look over your list of customers and principal buyers. Which ones are high-Is? What are the signs that tell you this?"

Dave knew that his best sales came from this group, so he wasn't at all surprised that his three wins were all high-Is. But, as he looked down the page, he got an uncomfortable feeling in the pit of his stomach, because he was sure that none of his active prospects were high-Is.

Client	Key Buyer	Status	Style	The Signs
Fasteners in a Snap	Jillian McFarland, Vice President of Administration	Win	I	• Suggested a face-to-face meeting after the first call • Focused on relationships • Found us more credible when she learned we had installed the system for two people she knew
Better Beverage Makers	Bob Scott, Chief Executive Officer	Win	I	• CEO really clicked with our VP of Services—same school, similar interests; frequently wanted to meet over lunch • Conversations frequently got into other topics, seldom stayed focused • Felt that our values were more in line with theirs

Client	Key Buyer	Status	Style	The Signs
Ebank Finances	Vance Paulson, Director of European Expansion Unit	Win	I	• Felt that a meeting in person would be better • Made small talk about his excitement regarding the upcoming move to open the new branch in Germany • Didn't want to delve into details

The High-S Style

Before going into the next style, the facilitator went through a quick closed-book review to confirm that the participants were retaining the information he had presented about the first two styles. Dave's team scored seven points, getting all questions correct. Yet, what was most remarkable to Dave was how easily he could recall the information, even though the facilitator was providing a lot of detail.

"We have already talked about the high-D and high-I styles," the facilitator said. "Now let's move on to the third major style in the DISC model. *S* stands for steadiness. High-Ss tend to be the stabilizing force within an organization. They tend to be dependable, loyal workers who prefer a stable, secure environment. They love to help.

"While the high-Ds are busting through the wall and the high-Is are cheering people on, the high-Ss are quietly at the wall lending people a hand, helping people over it. They're not the loud ones; they're not the ones making a lot of noise. For the person needing a boost, the high-Ss will supply it. For those needing a lift, the high-S will crouch down, link hands, and provide the lift. And, for those who need a step, some high-Ss will even get down in the mud on their hands and knees and allow you to step on their backs to help you over the wall.

"What are the classic occupations for high Ss? Social service workers, civil servants, retail clerks. What is the value to the organization of high-Ss? High-Ss tend to be supportive, dependable workers. They are people-oriented and good listeners. They are accommodating and tolerant of others. When high-Ds are being pushy and abrasive, high-Ss understand that this is just the way high-Ds are. When high-Is are blabbing away, high-Ss are there listening. They understand that high-Is can ramble sometimes. So high-Ss are dependable, tolerant, loyal workers.

"Unfortunately," the facilitator added, "they also have a downside. High-Ss can avoid dealing with issues until they become big problems. This happens because they really dislike confrontation. So, if you do something that upsets high-Ss, they will likely take it without saying or doing anything about it. And if you do something else that upsets high-Ss, again they will take it without saying or doing anything about it. Do something else, they will still take it. Do something else and they will explode. And when a high-S explodes, you really want to be somewhere else. When the frustration for high-Ss gets to be so great that they express it, watch out. Many of us might think, 'I don't understand, all I did was . . . ,' but what we don't see are all the things that have been building up.

"So, one downside of high-Ss is that they don't like confrontation and they will avoid dealing with problems. Another downside is that they can seem to lack vision and creativity. That's because they are trying to make things work while ensuring that everyone is comfortable. They tend not to be the ones thinking outside the box.

"And, finally, high-Ss can be slow to accept change and hold grudges. They want stability, not change. For classic high-Ss, change is a four-letter word—change is chaotic, decreases stability, and disrupts relationships.

"One of the reasons high-Ss dislike confrontation is because of their *key factor: being liked.* High-Ss want to be liked. They want harmony. They want everyone to get along.

"So how do you sell to a high-S?" The facilitator put up the following chart:

High-S Key Factor: Being Liked

Selling Do's	Selling Don'ts
1. Start with a personal comment.	1. Don't dive straight into business.
2. Present ideas deliberately and clearly; provide assurances.	2. Don't be demanding or abrasive.
3. Make sure they are in agreement before moving on.	3. Don't assume that "silence means consent."

"I want to talk a bit more about how high-Ss respond when someone is demanding or abrasive," the facilitator continued. "Let's do it by comparison. If a high-D is demanding and abrasive to another high-D, the other high-D will be demanding and abrasive back. If a high-D is demanding and abrasive to a high-I, the high-I will tell everyone how demanding and abrasive the high-D has been. The high-I will tell peers, co-workers, the spouse, the dog—anyone who will listen. Now, if a high-D is demanding and abrasive to a high-S, the high-S will shut down. The high-S will not say a thing. And this gets us to the final point. Don't assume that silence means consent. When high-Ss agree with you, they nod their heads. When they disagree, they do nothing. Be careful, you may miss it!

"So let's summarize. You can remember how to sell to high-Ss by keeping in mind this key phrase:

....
High-S: Start personal, don't assume.
....

Not bothering to raise his hand, Douglas, the bank branch manager, interrupted. "I don't get it. We're a bank. When people come to the bank, they want to transact business. What's wrong with diving straight into business? That's what they come to us to do."

The facilitator turned the question back to the group. "Who wants to take it? Who can explain why you shouldn't dive straight into business with a high-S?"

Sam, the telecommunications company sales rep, raised his hand. "Maybe this will help. For a high-S, when you start a conversation talking about business, it can suggest that the business is more important to you than the person. For some high-Ss, that can be a bit offensive."

A person from another table added, "That's exactly what is wrong with my bank. They send me stuff in the mail about new services to 'fit my needs,' but when I go in to talk with them, it's like I'm just a number. Totally impersonal."

Another person jumped in, "I've had that same problem with my bank. Every time I . . ."

The facilitator stepped in to cut off the discussion. "Let's slow down this train. We are not here to discuss how banks can be more relationship-oriented. Plus, it is always easier to focus on what *other people* should do to adjust to the buying styles of *their* customers. Let's get back to learning about buying styles so that we can all get better with our own customers.

"But, before we move on to the next style, look over your list of customers and principal buyers. Do you think any of your principal buyers are high-Ss? What are the signs that tell you this?"

Dave was now sure that the buyer he had dealt with in his most recent win with Fasteners in a Snap was a high-S, not a high-I. He could see that this person was focused on relationships, but at the same time she was quite reserved. Her questions always focused on people, and she was the one who suggested that they hold a face-to-face meeting after the initial call. Yet, his company had learned of a key concern she had from another department. She was reluctant to tell Dave directly. Dave also recalled that, in their last conversation, when he mentioned how CRM First could help her change and transform her department, she did not respond. At the time, Dave thought that meant agreement. But now, the facilitator's comment about change being a four-letter word for high-Ss had him doubting that assumption. In fact, the telecommunications rep on his team reminded Dave of this client. They both were likable but relatively reserved. This was in marked contrast to his other two high-I wins. Those two clients were highly gregarious, outgoing people. When Dave was with either of them, he had a hard time getting a word in.

Dave revised his information about Fasteners in a Snap, which now appeared as follows:

Client	Key Buyer	Status	Style	The Signs
Fasteners in a Snap	Jillian McFarland, Vice President of Administration	Win	S	• Suggested a face-to-face meeting after the first call • Focused on relationships • Found us more credible when she learned we had installed the system for two people she knew • Reserved in conversation • Was reluctant to tell us directly of a key concern she had; we learned of it from another department

The High-C Style

"We have talked about the high-D, high-I, and high-S styles," the facilitator said. "Let's move on to the last style in the DISC model, the high-C. *C* stands for Compliance. High-Cs tend to rely on rational logic and evidence to reach conclusions. They make sure that things are done by the book.

"While the high-Ds are busting through the wall, the high-Is are cheerleading, and the high-Ss are helping people over the wall, the high-Cs are doing their homework. First they measure the height of the wall and enter the information into their spreadsheet. Then they use the scaling equipment to determine that the wall is at an 84.5-degree angle. Next they check the wind speed and their own weight. And, finally, after entering all the data into the spreadsheet, they hit the 'calc' icon. The spreadsheet produces a four-page report that shows if they stand exactly 20 feet 5 inches from the wall, take seven strides averaging 2.7 feet each, and leap with a force equivalent to the correct proportion of their body mass, they will clear the wall by two inches and land 2.1 feet on the other side. And, if you have a few minutes, they would like to walk you through each detailed calculation.

"When you think of typical occupations for high-Cs, think of researchers, accountants, engineers, analysts, and people in other detailed or quantitative professions," the facilitator continued. "What's the value to the organization of high-Cs? High-Cs tend to be organized and detail-oriented. They make sure that decisions are well supported by facts and figures. They ensure that procedures are properly followed. It's the high-Cs who look for answers as to why things won't work. It's the high-Cs who help ensure that we maintain high quality. It's the high-Cs who help keep our processes efficient.

"Unfortunately, like all the other styles, high-Cs also have a downside. High-Cs can be perfectionists and very hard to please. Not only do they have high expectations for themselves, they tend to also have high expectations for those around them. And no one generally enjoys having to live up to someone else's high expectations.

"High-Cs can also be so focused on facts and figures that they ignore the people side, resulting in their sometimes being considered cold and calculating.

"Finally, high-Cs can be overly cautious and suffer from analysis paralysis—taking far too long to make even the smallest of decisions.

"Why do they do this? Because of their *key factor: getting it right.* High-Cs want to get it right. They would rather make no decision at all then make the wrong decision.

"So how do you sell to a high-C? It's not rocket science. You basically have to build a logical case that makes it obvious to them that they are making the right decision." The facilitator put up the following chart:

High-C Key Factor: Getting It Right

Selling Do's	**Selling Don'ts**
1. Present ideas in a logical fashion.	1. Don't be disorganized or make random comments.
2. Stay on topic.	2. Don't rely on emotional appeal to gain agreement.
3. Provide facts and figures that back up claims.	3. Don't force a rapid decision.

"If you are a salesperson used to winning people over with personality, charisma, relationship, or emotion, you can forget it. You will likely be highly ineffective with high-Cs. They want the facts and the figures. They expect you to ask the right questions, provide them with alternatives, do what you say you are going to do, and make no claims that you aren't able to immediately back up with evidence.

"To summarize, you can remember how to sell to this group by keeping in mind this key phrase for high-Cs:

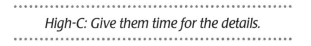

High-C: Give them time for the details.

Long before the facilitator asked them to take a look at their buyer list, Dave was already in pain. Clearly the buyer from Web Systems and Tools was a high-C. The evidence was very clear:

- She had no interest in relationship building. While his organization had wined and dined others involved in the sale, she had never participated.

- She was the one who had asked for the names of two competitors. Dave had thought it was a perfunctory move to meet her company's purchasing requirement. He had no idea she wanted confirmation that she was making the right choice.

- She always seemed a little irritated if they were a few minutes late for a meeting, which was often the case.

- And he remembered that when her organization had asked for additional information, as it had on several occasions, she had had to call him back twice because the information was not in the exact format she had requested.

And then Dave remembered one of the things she had said during the "you-didn't-win" call: "We just had a lot more confidence in the other team's ability to *follow through* and meet our needs." Ouch! It was so obvious why they hadn't won the work. Why hadn't he seen it before?

"Before we go any further, please go ahead and complete your buyer list. We have reviewed all four of the types. Where do you think your nine buyers fall?"

Dave completed his list, which now looked like this:

Client	Key Buyer	Status	Style	The Signs
Fasteners in a Snap	Jillian McFarland, Vice President of Administration	Win	S	• Suggested a face-to-face meeting after the first call • Focused on relationships • Found us more credible when she learned we had installed the system for two people she knew • Reserved in conversation • Was reluctant to tell us directly of a key concern; we learned of it from another department
Better Beverage Makers	Bob Scott, Chief Executive Officer	Win	I	• CEO really clicked with our VP of Services—same school, similar interests; frequently wanted to meet over lunch • Conversations frequently got into other topics, seldom stayed focused • Felt that our values were more in line with theirs
Ebank Finances	Vance Paulson, Director of European Expansion Unit	Win	I	• Felt that a face-to-face meeting would be better • Made small talk about his excitement regarding the upcoming move to open the new branch in Germany • Didn't want to delve into details

Client	Key Buyer	Status	Style	The Signs
Web Systems and Tools	Sharlene Case, Vice President of Administration and Technology	Loss	C	• Had no interest in relationship building • Asked for names of competitors to confirm that she was making the right choice • Seemed a little irritated if team was a few minutes late for a meeting
Global Tech Electronic Specialists	Myron Griffin, Senior Vice President	Loss	C	• Wanted us to provide the detail calculations demonstrating our cost-benefit analysis claim • Maintained a thoroughly organized office • Handed us a detailed format that we were to use for proposing
The Candy Company	Fiona Young, Vice President of Sales	Loss	D	• Wanted someone to "just get it done" • Had no interest in depth and breadth of features • Had unrealistic expectations on delivery time
Financial Compliance Advisers	Geoffrey Wilson, Chief Executive Officer	Active	C	• Seemed difficult to engage in casual conversation • Made three requests for revisions to our meeting agenda • Became overly agitated when the meal he ordered was not prepared to his specifications

(continued)

BAKER College of Clinton Twp LIBRARY

Client	Key Buyer	Status	Style	The Signs
Regent Imaging Corporation	Ross Studebaker, Chief Operating Officer	Active	D	• All meetings short and to the point • Pushed us down to work with lower people in his organization • When named head of the project midway through, did not review any of the previous documentation
Premier Granite and Tile	John Eric, Vice President of Operations	Active	C	• Insisted on having information sent to him and then requested additional information before agreeing to a meeting • Had read all the literature and was prepared with a detailed list of questions when we first met

"We are going to take a break here," the facilitator announced. "But before we do, take a minute each to share with your teammates answers to the following three questions:

1. Which style do you find it easiest to sell to, and why?

2. Which style do you find it most difficult to sell to, and why?

3. Given the three opportunities you are actively selling, what actions might you consider taking to make the buyers more comfortable?"

Dave was certainly in need of a break. The revelations over the past 90 minutes had come fast and furious, and he was feeling overwhelmed. What he didn't know was that the most important revelation for him would come right after the break.

CHAPTER 4

Selling to Your Boss

. . . .

"We have covered the four basic buying styles, and you have had a chance to reflect on the styles of accounts you have won, accounts you have lost, and accounts that you are currently attempting to sell," the facilitator began after the group had returned from its break. "I want to switch our topic from theory to application for a few minutes by looking at strategies for applying these principles. Let's start with a simple example of selling to your boss. Then we'll return to selling to your customers.

"Listen closely as I paint a scenario for you. A problem has arisen in your area. You have fully researched this problem and have created an eight-page document that defines the issue, identifies four possible alternatives for addressing the issue, and provides the strengths and weaknesses of each alternative. You favor alternative four. Note that you have done the 'high-C thing' very well!

"You are about to meet with your boss to talk about the problem and to sell your boss on how to solve it. Your boss knows nothing about the problem and is not anticipating your visit. You knock on the door. You hear, 'Come in.'

"Depending on your boss's buying style, what would be the first words out of your mouth? For example, if your boss is a high-D, what would be the first words you would say? What if your boss is a high-I, or a high-S, or a high-C? Think about what you have learned so far about the four buying styles, and think carefully about what individuals who buy in that style want you to do for them or what they want from you when you walk through the door. You will have eight minutes to work in your teams using new team leaders. I would like your four answers on a single flip chart page."

First Words

On Dave's team, it was Ian, the automobile sales manager, who led the team. "This could be a fun exercise. I took a class in Myers-Briggs a few years back, and we did something similar. Let's talk about the high-D style. What's the best way to communicate with them? Who has an idea?" Connie, the accounting executive, responded, "According to the directions, we are supposed to decide what our first words would be, presumably after we entered our boss's office. A high-D would not be interested in a lot of chitchat, so I think we should get right to the point by explaining the problem."

Douglas, the bank manager, responded, "That would never work. I think I'm a high-D, and I don't like talking about problems. I like hearing about solutions. So when you come into my office, I want to know what you think we should do. I want to hear, 'I think we need to do xyz and here's why.' That would work for me."

"Is everyone fine with that?" Ian asked.

"Works for me," Dave responded, with the rest of the team in agreement.

"What about the high-I?" Ian continued in his leadership role. "What would we want to say?"

"I think the same approach would work," said Douglas. "Just get to the point."

Dave took objection this time. "I think I'm a high-I, and I'm pretty sure that approach wouldn't work with me. You've got to get me warmed up a bit before I'm ready to dive into business. I would want you to——"

Ian interrupted him in midsentence. "See, I knew I liked you for a reason. I'm the same way. Everything doesn't have to be business all the time. Let's talk about the ball game last night, or ask me about my vacation or how the new hire is working out. Let's mix it up a bit."

"Exactly!" Dave responded. "Now that's the way to have a conversation and to build good business relationships at the same time."

"All right!" Ian said, giving Dave a high five across the table.

"When you two high-Is finish with the long-lost-brothers thing, would one of you tell us what to write? What should be the first words out of your mouth if your boss is a high-I?" asked Douglas.

"'How was your weekend?' sounds pretty good to me," Dave said.

"That works well," said Ian. "So let's move on to the high-S. Do we have any high-Ss on the team?"

Dave immediately turned to Sam, the telecommunications rep, who had been quiet up to this point. "I guess that would be me," Sam replied, though it sounded more like a question than a statement. "You all have been doing such a good job of figuring this out; I really didn't feel a need to say anything. I'm not sure I'm a high-S, but if you came into my office to discuss business, I think the right thing to do is to 'start personal' like the facilitator said, though not too personal. You might ask, 'How's the family?' or something like that. If you happen to remember my spouse's name or something personal from our last conversation, like where we were planning to go on vacation, that would be a good start. Overall, though, the point would be to start personal."

"So why don't we write, 'How's the family?'" Ian suggested.

"I'm okay with that," Sam answered.

"Are all Ss so touchy-feely?" Douglas asked, unsuccessfully hiding a tone of irritation in his voice.

"Are all high-Ds so abrasive?" Dave replied, with a laugh.

Ian jumped in. "Okay, that means we should move on to the high-Cs. How should we start the conversation with the high-Cs?"

Dave responded first. "Frankly, this is the hardest type for me to work with. If you all can give me insights, it would be a big help. They really do drive me crazy."

Sam spoke next. "Dave, if this helps, I think high-Cs can be pretty easy to get along with as long as I don't back them into a corner. I find that they just don't like being rushed into a decision. They want to have plenty of time to consider all the facts."

"So what does that mean in terms of what we say when we walk into our boss's office?" Douglas asked.

There were several seconds of silence until Connie, the accounting executive, spoke up. "Of the four types, I think I am more like a high-C than any of the others. If I'm your boss, what Sam says is more or less correct. I don't want to be rushed into a decision. You should carefully explain the problem to me and walk me through the four proposals. Then you need to give me time to reflect, to research other alternatives that I might want to consider, and then come to the best conclusion in the time we have."

"Two minutes remaining," the facilitator said from the front of the room.

"With more emphasis this time . . . so what does that mean in terms of what we say when we walk into our boss's office?" asked Douglas, feeling the time pressure.

"Please, let me think about it for a second, will you?" replied Connie.

"Douglas, we don't want to back our only high-C into a corner. We may need her later!" Ian quipped. "How would this feel?" he continued, "Suppose we write, 'We are having a problem, and I would like to walk you through some possibilities for how to solve it.' Is that a decent start?"

"Good start, but we have to get the time thing in there," said Dave. "Suppose we say, 'We are having a problem, and I would like to walk you through some possibilities for how to solve it. Do you have time now to talk?'"

"That's better," Ian said. "How does it feel to you, Connie?"

"I agree it is a decent start and may very well be the best we can do in this short time frame," Connie responded.

When they were done, the Red Team's chart appeared as follows:

The Red Team—First Words Out of Your Mouth

- D—I think we need to do xyz and here's why.
- I—How was your weekend?
- S—How's the family?
- C—We are having a problem, and I would like to walk you through some possibilities for how to solve it. Do you have time now to talk?

"I'm looking around the room at the flip charts," the facilitator began, "and I can tell that the teams all spent some quality time discussing this assignment and coming to some conclusions. Before we talk about the responses, let me ask you, did you notice any of the typical buying style behaviors or *dysfunctions* occurring within your team?" The facilitator's emphasis on the word "dysfunctions" sent chuckles throughout the room. It was pretty clear to Dave that the other teams must have had an experience similar to what had occurred in his team.

"We'll be talking later about some of the behaviors you observed," the facilitator said. "But let's get to the meat of the work for this module.

"Remember the scenario: A problem has arisen in your area. You have fully researched this problem and have created an eight-page document that describes this problem, identifies four possible alternatives, and analyzes the strengths and weaknesses of each. You favor alternative four. You are about to meet with your boss to talk about the problem and how to solve it. Your boss knows nothing about the problem and is not anticipating your visit. You knock on the door. You hear, 'Come in.' Depending on your boss's buying style, what would be the first words out of your mouth? Let's start with the high-D. Blue Team first: What did you say would be the first words out of your mouth?"

The four teams gave the following responses:

If Your Boss Is a High-D

Blue Team: We're having a problem with . . . can you take time now to talk about it?

Green Team: Do you have a minute to talk about how to handle a problem we're having with . . .?

Red Team: I think we need to do xyz, and here's why.

Black Team: I need ten minutes to get your decision on . . . is now good?

"There are several good responses here, but there is one that is clearly the strongest if we draw on our understanding of how to work successfully with high-Ds. I think you will see why. Remember the hint I gave you. Ask yourself this question: When you walk through the door, what does the high-D want from you? Recall that the key factor for high-Ds is time—don't waste their time! So when you walk through the door, high-D prospects and customers want you to tell them two things in particular: What do you want, and how much of their time are you going to use?

"So if you say, 'We're having a problem with . . . do you have time now to talk about it?,' you have answered one of their questions—what do you want?—but you haven't answered the question about time. You haven't told them how much time you need, and therefore they can't judge whether the discussion is worth the investment. In addition, high-Ds, as a general rule, don't want to 'talk about problems.' Their preference is to focus on solutions.

"If you say, 'Do you have a minute to talk about how to handle a problem we're having with . . .?,' once more there is the issue with discussing problems instead of solutions.

"Also," the facilitator continued, "high-Ds know that few discussions take a minute. So a very high-D might be a bit perturbed that you are starting by implying that you need only a minute when this is likely not the truth.

"If you say, 'I think we need to do xyz, and here's why,' you are focusing on approval, which is good, but you still have the time issue.

"But if you start the discussion by saying, 'I need ten minutes to get your decision on . . .,' you have made it clear to them what you want, you have phrased it as a decision—which they like discussing—rather than as a problem, and you have been clear how much time you require. High-Ds will love and respect you for this."

Dave saw heads nodding all around the room. It made sense. Of course that was a better way to start the conversation with high-Ds.

"By thinking about what the style wants from you, you can get a better idea for how to start the conversation in a way that works for that person's style," the facilitator said.

"So let's look at the other three styles. What does a high-I want from you when you walk through the door, and what might be appropriate first words?"

When the facilitator finished his discussion of the four buying styles, he had created a flip chart which contained the following information:

What They Want from You	First Words Out of Your Mouth
D They want to know what you want and how much time it is going to take.	I need ten minutes to get your decision on . . .
I They want the stage.	How was your weekend?
S They want a friendly interaction.	How are you?
C They want time for the details.	*(Send e-mail ahead of time with details.)* If now is good, I would like to take as much time as you need to discuss the problem we are having with . . .

The High-D Conversation

"We've talked about the first words out of your mouth. Now let's talk about the rest of the conversation with your boss. Take a look at the chart I'm putting up. I want each of you to take four minutes individually to complete it. Decide, for each style, which of the activities you would do first, second, third, and so on. Notice that not every activity will necessarily be done for each of the styles. Start with the high-D column. Decide which activity you would do first, second, third, and so forth. You have four minutes."

	D	**I**	**S**	**C**
A. Pleasantries				
B. Explanation of the problem B1. High-level explanation				
B2. Detailed explanation				
C. Asking how to solve the problem				
D. Offering solution(s) D1. High-level explanation				
D2. Detailed explanation				
E. Benefits of solution(s) E1. Asking for the benefits				
E2. Explaining the benefits				
F. Reaching agreement on next step				

After four minutes, the facilitator continued the discussion. "Let's review the chart together. If your boss is a high-D and you are having the conversation we just talked about, where would you start first? Pleasantries? Absolutely not; not with a high-D. High-level explanation of the problem? Nope, not there, either. With high-Ds, you start with the solution. High-Ds are the type that often read the end of a book first and then decide whether or not they want to read the rest.

"After starting with the solution, from there you give a high-level explanation of the problem, describe the benefits of the solution, and then reach agreement on the next steps to take.

In essence, the conversation is, 'I would like to do . . ., because it solves these problems . . ., and as a result we get these benefits . . . can I get your approval to act?'"

	D	I	S	C
A. Pleasantries				
B. Explanation of the problem B1. High-level explanation	2			
B2. Detailed explanation				
C. Asking how to solve the problem				
D. Offering solution(s) D1. High-level explanation	1			
D2. Detailed explanation				
E. Benefits of solution(s) E1. Asking for the benefits				
E2. Explaining the benefits	3			
F. Reaching agreement on next step	4			

"With high-Ds, do you describe all four solutions? No, just the one you think is the best. But be prepared with the others, in case the high-D doesn't like your first solution.

The High-I Conversation

"Let's move on to the high-I. Where do you start? With pleasantries? Of course. And you want to be prepared, because your boss may want to spend quite some time on this. After giving your boss the stage, you are ready to transition to the second step, a high-level explanation of the problem. The next step is the critical one. What do you do next?"

Dave knew the answer, but a person from the Blue Team responded first. "Offer your solution?"

"This might be effective for some high-Is," the facilitator responded, "but the classic high-I prefers a different approach. Are there any people in the room who think they are high-Is?

More than half the hands went up. By the murmurs through the class, it was evident to Dave that many were surprised by this. Not Dave. *Of course, more than half the hands went up*, he thought. *This* is *a sales class.*

"So those who have your hands raised shout out the letter of the next step," said the facilitator. In near unison, "C" was shouted throughout the room.

Connie raised her hand. "Let me get this straight. Let's say I spend days researching a problem and prepare an eight-page report that identifies four solutions and analyzes the strengths and weaknesses of each. Now are you telling me that I am supposed to ask my boss how to solve this problem after she has spent perhaps five minutes listening to me describe it? How much sense does that make?"

"You're right, of course," the facilitator answered. "To someone who may be a high-C, asking a high-I how to solve the problem makes no sense at all. But to a high-I it makes perfect sense. Who can explain why?"

Ian offered his thoughts. "See, for me and many other high-Is, the fun part is in brainstorming solutions. So give us a problem and let us have fun with it. Give us some time to think about how we would solve it. We really don't want to hear your solution yet. We wouldn't want your thoughts to hamper our creativity!"

"Spoken like a true high-I," the facilitator said, adding, "And consider this. What would happen if you took this same step with a high-D? What would happen if you asked a high-D how to solve the problem?"

A member of the Green Team responded. "My boss is a high-D, and I can hear him now: 'Excuse me. Are you asking me how to solve *your* problem? Are you saying I have to do my job and *your* job, too? If that's what you are saying, then we probably don't need both of us, do we?'" Laughter filled the room.

"Yes, if your boss is a high-D, asking him or her how to solve the problem could be a major C.L.M.—a career-limiting move. But let's keep going," the facilitator said.

"For high-Is, step 1 is pleasantries, step 2 is a high-level explanation of the problem, and step 3 is asking them how to solve the problem. In step 4, you describe the solution you want. Once more, you describe *only* the solution you want, not the others. Step 5 is an interesting one. Remember the shorthand for dealing with the high-I: *Let them sell themselves.* This is exactly what happens in step 5: You ask the high-I to describe the benefits of your solution. They are now describing what they like about what you are suggesting. Finally, there's step 6, and you get an agreement to move forward. So let's recap the high-I."

With the recap, the facilitator showed the chart completed for the first two styles:

	D	I	S	C
A. Pleasantries		1		
B. Explanation of the problem B1. High-level explanation	2	2		
B2. Detailed explanation				
C. Asking how to solve the problem		3		
D. Offering solution(s) D1. High-level explanation	1	4		
D2. Detailed explanation				
E. Benefits of solution(s) E1. Asking for the benefits		5		
E2. Explaining the benefits	3			
F. Reaching agreement on next step	4	6		

The High-S Conversation

The facilitator continued. "How about the high-S? This is perhaps the simplest of the style conversations. You start with pleasantries, of course. Then, as you can see from the chart, the flow is very much like telling a story: a high-level explanation of the problem, a high-level explanation of the solution you prefer, an explanation of the benefits of the solution proposed, and a request for an agreement to move forward. High-Ss will be able to follow your flow, and, if the solution makes sense to them and takes into account concerns about people, they will tend to go along with you.

	D	I	S	C
A. Pleasantries		1	1	
B. Explanation of the problem B1. High-level explanation	2	2	2	
B2. Detailed explanation				
C. Asking how to solve the problem		3		
D. Offering solution(s) D1. High-level explanation	1	4	3	
D2. Detailed explanation				
E. Benefits of solution(s) E1. Asking for the benefits		5		
E2. Explaining the benefits	3		4	
F. Reaching agreement on next step	4	6	5	

The High-C Conversation

"Now we come to the high-Cs. Recall that you will have done well to have e-mailed the document to the high-C in advance. So where do you start when your boss is a high-C? With pleasantries? Of course not. High-Cs have little interest in the so-called touchy-feely stuff. Start first with a high-level explanation of the problem. Are you done? Absolutely not. You will then need to go into a detailed explanation. See, you have to convince a high-C that there really is a problem that needs solving. You have to explain what the problem is, how big it is, how long it has been occurring, its root cause, its cost to the organization, and so on.

"Once you have convinced a high-C that there is a problem and that the problem is worth solving, you give a high-level explanation of the solutions, followed by a detailed review of each of the solutions you analyzed, including the strengths and weaknesses of each. You then explain the benefits and ask if the high-C is ready to make a decision or if additional information is needed."

The facilitator showed the following chart with all four styles completed:

	D	I	S	C
A. Pleasantries		1	1	
B. Explanation of the problem B1. High-level explanation	2	2	2	1
B2. Detailed explanation				2
C. Asking how to solve the problem		3		
D. Offering solution(s) D1. High-level explanation	1	4	3	3

	D	**I**	**S**	**C**
D2. Detailed explanation				4
E. Benefits of solution(s) E1. Asking for the benefits		5		
E2. Explaining the benefits	3		4	5
F. Reaching agreement on next step	4	6	5	6

A hand went up from a member of the Black Team, who asked, "You said we would have to walk through a detailed explanation of all four alternatives. Why do this? Isn't this a waste of time if alternative four is the obvious answer?"

"Another fair question," said the facilitator. "Who can tell me why it is important to walk through the details of all four alternatives?"

Connie was on this one. "You have to show the high-Cs that you have done your homework. You have to show them that you have thought through the alternatives, and you have to explain why you have chosen the one you have over the others. By doing this, you give them the assurance that they can trust your conclusions."

It was like a bell went off in Dave's head. Without realizing he was speaking out loud, he found himself saying, "That's it. That's what I've been missing about high-Cs. You said, 'By *doing* this, you give them the assurance that they can trust your conclusions.'"

"It sounds like someone on the Red Team has had a bit of an epiphany," the facilitator pointed out. "Dave, can you speak louder so that everyone else can share in it?"

Dave started in. "As I've been going through this morning, it has become painfully obvious that I win most of the time when I am selling to high-Is, my own style, and that I lose frequently when I sell to high-Cs. As if this weren't bad enough, of the three prospects on the list I brought to the class, the principal buyers for two of them appear to be high-Cs. I mentioned earlier to my team that this is the group to whom I need to learn to sell better. And when Connie made her last comment, 'By doing this, you give them the assurance that they can trust your conclusions,' the problem I am having has become very clear.

"See, when I provide assurances to my high-I clients, they trust my assurances because they trust me. With high-Cs, the way they will trust my assurances is not through their relationship with me but by the things I do—following through, providing details, *doing* the things that show them that they can trust my assurances. Getting the details right has never been my forte. My motto has been 'Roughly right is right enough.' In fact, my tendency has been to blow off the details and put these things near the bottom of the list. I can see how high-Cs could think that, in essence, I was blowing *them* off and that I was not concerned about the things that were important to them.

"I hope you are going to give us some tips for how to do this stuff better," Dave added. "I've been in sales for more than 25 years, and I'm feeling awfully ill equipped right now."

"Let me assure you that you will be walking from this session with strategies, Dave," the facilitator responded. "The point of this segment is to get each of you ready for the second half of the day. Given your comments, Dave, you get to move to the head of the class!"

Which Conversation?

"Now I have a question for everyone," the facilitator said. "I would bet that at least 75 percent of the people in this room have the same conversation with their boss. Which conversation is it, though? Is it the high-D, the high-I, the high-S, or the high-C?" Dave was sure that he knew the answer. At least, he thought he was sure.

"How many of you would say the conversation most of the people have with their boss is the high-D conversation?" the facilitator continued. About 30 percent of the room raised their hands.

"No, it's not the high-D conversation," said the facilitator. "How many would say the high-I conversation?" About 40 percent of the room raised their hands.

"No, it's not the high-I conversation either. How many would say it's the high-S conversation?" Only about 10 percent raised their hands.

"No, it's not the high-S conversation. How many would say the high-C conversation?" Dave could see that some people were not committing, as only a few more hands went up. When the facilitator told them that it was not the high-C conversation, murmurs went through the room.

"If it's not the high-D, I, S, or C, then what is it?" Douglas asked.

"It's *our* conversation," the facilitator answered. "The tendency for each of us is to have *our* conversation with the boss. If we are a high-D, we tend to try to have the high-D conversation with the boss. If we are a high-I, we tend to have the high-I conversation. If we are a high-S or high-C, it is the same thing. We all tend to try to have *our* conversation with the boss. But what conversation should we be having?"

"*Their* conversation," was the unison response by many in the room.

"That's right," said the facilitator. "We should be having the boss's conversation. Why? Because if we have that conversation, the boss will be able to better hear us and understand us. This is one clear sign of effective communicators. They understand the importance of communicating in the other person's style so that the person will hear them. Yet, in most conversations, a battle is being waged. Each person is fighting to have his or her *own* conversation.

"Let me give you an example of what I mean. Imagine a high-C having the conversation we've been talking about with his boss, a high-D. I think it would sound like this."

> *Effective communicators understand the importance of communicating in the other person's style.*

The facilitator role-played the conversation with a member of the Blue Team, with the facilitator playing the high-D:

A Typical Conversation

High-C: I sent you an eight-page document describing a problem we are having and four potential alternatives for addressing it. Did you have a chance to—

(The high-D interrupts the high-C in midsentence.)

High-D: Right, I remember that long e-mail. I haven't had a chance to look at it. Why don't you net it out for me? What is it that you think we should do, and why?

High-C: Let me start with the problem. I was doing some research last week, and, while reviewing customer complaint data, I noticed a significant increase in the percentage of complaints related to a specific part. Over the past two years, fewer than 1 percent of our complaints were about this same part. Last month, though, 15 percent of the complaints had to do with the part. And, when I looked back at the prior month, it was 11 percent, and the month before it was 7 percent, and the— *(Again, the high-D interrupts the high-C in midsentence.)*

High-D: Okay, I get it. There's been an increase in the problem. What's the problem, and what do you want to do about it?

High-C: I just want to make sure that you understood this has been an increasing issue and that it is important we solve it before it gets any worse. The problem is that we are experiencing failures with part number K75226, which, as you know, we import from a Korean manufacturer. When we were looking for a manufacturer for this part several years ago, it had come down to this vendor and one other. We chose this vendor because of its track record of higher quality. When I talked with the Korean manufacturer, the rep told me . . .

(By this time the high-D has determined he is not going to get the information he wants from the high-C quickly. Therefore, while the high-C continues to go into detail, the high-D finds and opens the e-mail and scans the document. The high-D interrupts again.)

High-D: I see your analysis of the problem here. It looks like you isolated it to be a manufacturing issue, and you have identified four recommendations. Your preferred recommendation is to have the manufacturer pay for a recall of all parts manufactured over the past six months. I'm fine with that as long as we make the recall voluntary for our customers.

High-C: After careful consideration, I do believe this to be our best alternative. But I think it would make sense for us to take some time to examine the other three alternatives because they have strengths, as well.

High-D: I see your strengths and weaknesses here. I can't think of anything you may have missed. I'm fine with what we've just discussed. You should bring me in again only if the manufacturer balks at the recall. Anything else? Otherwise, I need to get back to work.

"Could you see the conversation battle?" the facilitator asked. "How often do you think this happens in everyday conversations in organizations around the world? Now think about how this same conversation must play out in sales situations every single day—situations in which salespeople are trying to sell in their style and buyers are trying to buy in theirs."

Dave noticed a hand go up from someone on the Green Team. "Excuse me," the participant said. "You gave us an example of a dysfunctional conversation, which I guess is typical of many conversations. But, if each person understood buying styles, how would the conversation have been different? If the high-C was trying to communicate like the high-D and the high-D was trying to communicate like the high-C, wouldn't it still be a dysfunctional conversation?"

"Good question," the facilitator responded. "Let's find out. I would like to get two volunteers to role-play the conversation. I would like to get someone who believes he or she may be a high-D to play that role. And I would like to have someone who believes he or she may have high-C tendencies to play the high-C role. The objective of the role play is to do the best you can to communicate with the other person in that person's style. Do I have volunteers for the high-C and the high-D?"

Dave wasn't surprised to see Douglas raise his hand to play the high-D. But he was very surprised to find that Connie volunteered to be the high-C. And, when the conversation started, he was equally surprised at how well each did. Everyone laughed when Connie started the conversation with the same language identified during the class:

A Better Conversation

Connie: Do you have ten minutes? I need to get your approval to take action on solving the problem we're having with part K75226.

Douglas: Actually, I am a little pressed at the moment. But if you can bring me up to speed on the problem in eight minutes, we can schedule a follow-up if we need more time. Tell me what's going on.

Connie: Let me start with my end point first. I believe we should ask for the Korean manufacturer of part K75226 to recall all parts manufactured over the past six months. The reason for the recall is that this part has gone from being the focus of fewer than 1 percent of our total complaints two years ago to 7 percent, 11 percent, and, most recently, 15 percent over the past three months. The manufacturer has isolated the problem, and if it agrees to recall the defective part, we would then let our clients know we are being proactive in solving a problem that they may not have even been aware of. This will help us to continue to build trusting relationships with our client base. Assuming we can get the manufacturer to agree, does this meet with your approval?

Douglas: It sounds like you've done a great job of researching this. I like it. We should, however, make the recall voluntary for our customers. But let me ask you: Are there other alternatives we should be considering, as well?

Connie: I did analyze three other alternatives and identified the strengths and weaknesses of each. I believe the one we have discussed is the best of the group, but, if you would like, I can go over the others with you and discuss their strengths and weaknesses.

Douglas: No, that won't be necessary. But why don't you put those alternatives into an e-mail for me in case we need to come back to this? Assuming the Korean manufacturer doesn't balk at the recall, do we need to meet again on this, or are you comfortable we have given it the time needed to come to a reasonable solution?

Connie: No, I think we are fine. Thanks! I'll let you get back to work.

The other participants gave Douglas and Connie loud applause. "You two make it look easy," the facilitator said. "How was it for you?"

"It was a little uncomfortable, but not that hard at all," Douglas responded.

"What about you, Connie?" asked the facilitator.

"I'm not usually the volunteer type," Connie responded, "but I had promised myself before this seminar that I was going to do my best to get as much out of it as possible. I had a few jitters to start, but when people laughed after my first comment I found it easier to get into the role play. The big thing for me was to keep thinking, 'Get to the point. Keep it brief.' That seemed to work pretty well."

Douglas jumped in. "You're right, Connie. I hadn't realized it until you said it. During the entire conversation I kept thinking, 'Is this the right thing to do? Do we need more detail?' This is very interesting. Is that the trick? Is the way to have the other person's conversation to keep in your head the shorthand you talked about?"

"Some have said that it is helpful to keep a reminder in front of them of the shorthand," the facilitator responded. "But different strategies work for different people. The overall idea is to keep in your mind what the other person wants. This will help you be a more effective communicator *and* a more effective salesperson.

"We need to move on to talk about how to identify the buying styles of others. But, before we do, I would like to give you a few minutes to think about this exercise. Think about your own boss. Take a minute to jot down a few thoughts about him or her. What do you think your boss's style might be? Then, given this presumed style, jot down some steps you might take to communicate with and sell to your boss more effectively in the future."

CHAPTER 5

Identifying the Buying Styles of Others

Having understood the behaviors of people with each of the four buying styles covered earlier in the morning, Dave felt fairly confident he could assess their styles once he started working with them. For him, the high-Ds and high-Cs were especially easy to identify. The high-Ds would always try to take control of the conversation. The high-Cs would be the data gatherers. They would always want more information. The high-Is and high-Ss were a little harder for him to distinguish. They both were very friendly. The high-Is, however, were those who tended to have even more to say than Dave did, while the high-Ss would be more content to listen.

Though comfortable with figuring out their buying styles once he worked with people for a while, Dave wanted to get to the point where he could assess a style early in the first meeting. He also knew he needed better strategies for adapting.

"We've covered a lot of ground already today," said the facilitator. "We've talked about the four basic buying styles, and we've used the example of selling to your boss to identify how important it is to adapt your style to the style of your audience. All this information has prepared us to focus on how to identify the buying styles of other people."

The Dimensions

"To identify the styles of people," the facilitator continued, "we look across the two dimensions shown on the screen, direct versus indirect and task-oriented versus people-oriented.

"Let's first talk about the direct–indirect dimension. Let's say you are giving a presentation and someone has a question about what you're saying. People who are more direct in their orientation will ask the question as soon as it occurs to them. People who are more indirect will likely wait until you finish, perhaps being more courteous to you or perhaps expecting that you will cover their question as you go along.

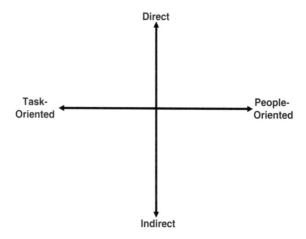

"Consider how direct-oriented people walk. They tend to walk with purpose. They have somewhere they're going. They look straight ahead and march to that place. On the other hand, people who are indirect will likely take their time, pause to take in the scenery, and enjoy the journey. It is a different orientation.

"The other dimension is task-oriented versus people-oriented," the facilitator explained. "Those who are task-oriented concentrate on getting the job done. Their focus is on activities and accomplishments. Those who are people-oriented are more interested in relationships. They focus on people and the impact decisions have on people. Again, it is a different orientation.

"As an example, assume your sales manager has been on vacation for two weeks. On her first day back at the office, she sees you walking down the hall. If she is people-oriented, what might be the first words out of her mouth?"

"How are you doing? How's your family?" answered a person from the Blue Team.

"That's right," said the facilitator. "She would want to get an update on what is happening with you and your life. Now, if she were task-focused, what would be the first words out of her mouth?"

Ian answered first. "How is that big sales opportunity going? What's the status? Anything I need to be aware of?"

"Exactly," said the facilitator. "Once more, it is a different orientation. So let's go back to the chart. People who are direct and task-oriented tend to communicate like high-Ds. People who are direct and people-oriented tend to communicate like high-Is. High-Ss tend to be people-oriented and indirect, and high-Cs tend to be indirect and task-oriented."

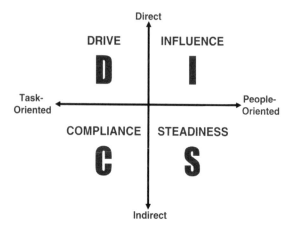

"I'm sure this is interesting to some. But my question is, how do I apply it?" asked Douglas.

"Let me answer your question," the facilitator said, "by using you as an example, Douglas. Red Team, get me started. On the basis of how you have experienced Douglas today, would you say Douglas is direct or indirect?"

Connie jumped in first. "Well, he did just ask a question and didn't wait for you to get to it. That sounds pretty direct to me."

"Okay," said the facilitator. "And does he seem to be task-oriented or people-oriented?"

"Task," said Dave. "*Way* over on the task side. He's the one who keeps bringing us back to the work."

"Direct and task-oriented—this would suggest that your primary buying style is high-D, Douglas," the facilitator concluded. "What do you think?"

"Of course I'm a high-D," Douglas responded. "But high-Ds are easy to spot. Let's take someone else."

"Okay," said the facilitator, "but, rather than taking someone in the class who people may not know as well, let's apply the dimensions to people with whom we are all probably familiar—U.S. presidents.

"Green Team, George H. W. Bush—the first Bush president—would you say he was direct or indirect? When there was a problem, would he attack it head-on, or would he want to wait and study it before deciding?"

A member of the Green Team piped in. "Definitely indirect. He never wanted to act hastily."

"Okay," the facilitator said. "Was he more people-focused or task-focused?"

"The man headed the CIA," another Green Team member jumped in. "Isn't that about as task-focused and indirect as you can get? That would make him a high-C."

"Okay," said the facilitator, "Blue Team, what about Bill Clinton. Direct or indirect? People-oriented or task-oriented?"

When the discussion was completed, the teams had concluded the following:

U.S. President	Dimension 1	Dimension 2	Style
George H. W. Bush	Indirect	Task-focused	High-C
Bill Clinton	Direct	People-focused	High-I
Jimmy Carter	Indirect	People-focused	High-S
George W. Bush	Direct	Task-focused	High-D

The Answering Machine

· ·

"We have talked about people we all know. But what about people we don't know? Well, there is some really good news when it comes to identifying the style of others. Put simply: People leak. They are leaking hints to you all the time as to how they want you to communicate with them. All you have to do is pay attention and look for the signs. Let's take an example of the answering machine.

"You call someone on the phone and you get his answering machine and you hear, 'You know what to do. Beep.' Now, which style is that?"

Dave laughed along with everyone else, including Douglas.

"This person is clearly saying, 'I'm a high-D," the facilitator continued. "Communicate with me like a high-D: Be prepared, be brief, be gone!' You didn't even get the person on the phone. You got his answering machine. In fact, he said just five words. But in those five words, there are hints that tell you to communicate with this person like a high-D.

"Let's take a second one. You get the answering machine and you hear, 'I'm sorry we're not here to take your call right now. But your call is very important to us. Please leave your message, and we will get back with you as soon as possible. Have a nice day.' Which style is this?"

Dave had never thought about how something as simple as a telephone greeting can quickly and easily tell you the person's preferred buying style. The cue phrases such as "I'm sorry" and "very important to us" seem to shout out a high-S mantra: "Relate to me! You're a person. I'm a person. Let's treat each other kindly."

"How about this one," the facilitator said. "You call someone, and the answering machine picks up and you hear, 'No one is available to take your call at the moment. At the sound of the tone, please leave your name, telephone number, the date and time of your call, and a brief explanatory message, and I will get back to you at the earliest possible convenience.' Which style?"

Something as simple as a telephone greeting can quickly and easily tell you the person's preferred buying style.

Connie laughed and said just loud enough for her table mates to hear, "That sounds similar to the message on my answering machine."

"And finally," the facilitator said, "The telephone rings, and when the answering machine picks up you hear eight seconds of music, followed by a bright and energetic 'No one's here right now. Leave a message!' Once more, the message shouts out, 'I'm a high-I! Communicate with me in a high-I style.'"

The Office

"Let's take a different example," the facilitator said. "Remember our initial point—being able to identify styles if you know what you are looking for. Let's go to the Black Team this time. If you walk into someone's office and you see a wall full of awards, plaques, certificates, and other items indicating the person's accomplishments, which style would you think that person is most likely?"

"Probably a high-D," answered the computer hardware saleswoman. "I have a few clients just like that. It's almost like they're saying, 'See what I've done. I'm better than you.'"

Dave looked over at Douglas, thinking he might have trouble letting that comment slide. Sure enough, Douglas jumped in.

"That's not it at all. I have plaques on my wall at work. I won them several years ago when I was a customer care rep for the bank. Five times I won highest regional sales. I just want my people to know they are working for someone who has done their job successfully."

A pharmaceutical salesperson from the Green Team jumped in. "I call on doctors every day, all of whom have plaques and certificates on the wall. But many of these doctors are high-Cs and high-Ss, and a few seem like they are high-Is. Just because someone has plaques on the wall doesn't mean that person is a high-D, does it?"

"Another very good point," said the facilitator. "Plaques don't necessarily mean high-D. They are just a sign to be aware of and another piece of input, just like the answering machine and the other information we will be talking about a little later. But it is important to be able to recognize the likely signs and to be able to adapt on the basis of the conclusions you reach and to readjust if the person's behavior tells you that you are selling in the wrong style.

"So, we've talked about the high-D's office. What about the high-I's office? What would you expect to see? Let's go to the Red Team for this answer. I'd like to start with Ian and go around to the left."

"Picking first on one of the high-Is in the group, are you?" Ian said, laughing. "Okay, judging from my office, you would probably see pictures with inspirational messages like 'Teamwork' and 'Success.'"

Several people in the room smiled and nodded in agreement with Ian's comment. But Connie didn't notice. She was studying the facilitator. Connie was married to a trainer who often talked with her about his work and the strategies he used to manage the classroom. Connie was fascinated with the various approaches this facilitator used to keep the group engaged. Yet, she had noticed that Sam seldom spoke during the full class discussions and wondered if the facilitator would notice in a class of 20 people. When she heard the facilitator say, ". . . start with Ian and go around to the left," Connie recognized the "mini-round-robin" technique as a vehicle for getting Sam involved without appearing to put him on the spot.

"Let's keep going around the team," the facilitator said. "Sam, you're next. Anything to add about what you would expect to see in the office of high-Is?"

"There might be a lot of distractibles," Sam said.

"Distractibles? I'm not sure I'm familiar with that term," the facilitator said.

"Things like cush balls for squeezing, or the basketball goal over the trash can, or the balls on the string that clang against each other. You know, distractibles—fun things that help spark their creativity, relieve stress, or reduce their boredom with a detailed task," Sam explained.

"Got it. Distractibles. That makes sense. Anything else, anyone?"

By the end of the discussion, the flip chart included the following information:

Office

D Awards, plaques, successes, last item worked on still on the desk

I Motivational pictures, distractibles, desk disorganized with information from multiple projects

S Pictures of family and friends, personal treasured items, atmosphere like someone's living room

C Either immaculate organization (e.g., desk clear, books lined up on shelves, typed file folder labels) or organized chaos (e.g., stacks of paper everywhere, but every stack having a purpose and specific information)

The Retail Store

The facilitator continued. "Let's take the scenario that you are a salesperson in a retail store and a male customer walks in. Let's assume that the customer has exhibited behaviors that suggest he is a high-D. What might those behaviors be for the retail store environment?"

"That's easy," said the sales manager from the retail clothing chain. "We get that type all the time. They either come right up to you and tell you what they are looking for, or they walk in, stop, gaze over the store as if they are viewing their kingdom, then go directly to what they want. They are not browsers. They want to get in, get what they want, and get out."

"Okay, what if the customer is a high-I?" asked the facilitator. "What would a high-I likely do when she walked into the retail store?"

The real estate agent from the Black Team spoke up. "I think the typical high-I would smile, make eye contact, and come over and start talking with you as if she had known you all your life. In the real estate market I deal a lot with couples. Sometimes the husband is a high-I, but most often it is the wife who speaks first and seems to have the higher I."

"Okay," the facilitator said, "that's the high-D and the high-I. Let's move on to the high-S. What would the person likely do when he walked through the door if he was a high-S?"

"For me that is the hardest one to decipher," said Douglas. "Sometimes they are friendly, like high-Is, and other times they are data gatherers like high-Cs. They confuse me."

"Who can help here?" asked the facilitator. After a few seconds of silence, Connie stepped in, "I think it is like you said. High-Ss are indirect and people-oriented. But they also want to avoid conflict. They would feel bad if you spent time with them and then they didn't buy anything. At the same time, they don't want to buy something that they don't really want. So, even though they are generally friendly, when they walk into the store they will likely want to avoid you because they don't want to feel pressured, by you or by themselves, to buy something."

"That's quite an insightful comment," said the facilitator. "And, as Connie has said, while they are friendly, when they walk into a store their conflict-avoidance tendency can kick in. So typical high-Ss may not make eye contact with you and may not come up to you unless they sense that you are warm and have a low-key sales approach. At the same time, high-Ss are loyal shoppers. If you treat them well and can gain their trust, they will come back again and again.

"So finally," said the facilitator, "let's talk about the high-C. As you might imagine, when high-Cs walk into a retail store, they walk in prepared. They typically already know exactly what they are seeking. If it is a grocery store, they will likely have a list carefully made out and double-checked. If they are walking into an appliance store, they will likely have the latest online product comparison matrix and detailed printouts of the options. They would prefer not to have to deal with a salesperson if they don't have to. So they will be a little annoyed if your store doesn't have the proper signage to indicate where they need to go to find what they want. If your store does have the signage, you will find them carefully reading the boxes and the specification sheets for each of the models they are considering. Because High-Cs want to be sure they are making the right decision, they will be there digesting the information your store makes available.

"Okay, let's review quickly some tips for recognizing each of the types when they walk into the store," the facilitator told the group, pulling out the following chart:

Walk into a Store

D • Comes right up to you and tells you what they are looking for
  • Or gazes over the store then go directly to what they want

I • Smiles and makes eye contact with you
  • Comes over and starts talking with you as if they had known you all your life

S • Generally doesn't make eye contact with you unless they know you

- Avoids you if they perceive you as cold or pushy

C
- Generally has a checklist or information to support their purchase
- Prefers not to be engaged unless you can provide them information they want

Buying Styles in the General Population

"I have a question," said a person from the Blue Team. "I help nonprofit organizations raise money, and I can readily see why I tend to be more successful with high-Ss, since they like supporting people and generally don't feel good when they have to say no to helping those in need. But my question is this: In the general population, what percentage of the people are high-Ss, high-Ds, and so on?"

"From a buying styles perspective, you just might be in the right business," the facilitator replied. "In a 2006 random sample of more than a quarter of a million people, 45 percent were high-Ss, 29 percent were high-Is, 18 percent were high-Ds, and 8 percent were high-Cs.

"Keep in mind that this was a random sample," he continued. "It is not unusual for your population of buyers to be different from these percentages. For example, if you sell to heads of engineering departments, you might find that this population of buyers has a heavier concentration of high-Cs than you would find in the general population. Likewise, if you sell predominantly to salespeople, you might find a higher percentage of high-Is among your buyers. Of course, you also have engineers who are high-Is and salespeople who are high-Cs. So avoid assuming a particular person's buying style solely on the basis of his or her title or position."

Pigeonholing?

A hand went up from the Green Team. It was the sales manager from the clothing store. "This feels a lot like we are pigeonholing people. You said up front that each one of us has some level of all four styles in us. We are all very complex. How could it possibly make sense to try to fit each person in the world into one of these four buckets?"

"Another excellent question. Does anyone want to take it?" Connie noted that no hands went up immediately. But, rather than responding, the facilitator continued to look around the room. Connie was curious about what the facilitator was doing. She smiled to herself when Sam's hand went up.

"Yes, we are all individuals," Sam said, "and very complex. But I can see how this would be a tool for helping us sell more effectively to people just by having an idea of how to sell to them. If more salespeople just knew what to look for, it would make a difference. Earlier today, the facilitator offered an example from his personal life of a time when a friend tried to sell him insurance and the salesperson insisted on selling in his own style. I've had the same experience when my wife and I were picking out the light fixtures for our new house. The salesperson was a high-I and wouldn't stop talking. I didn't so much have a problem with it. But my wife is a high-D with some high-C. This salesperson's style drove her nuts. The only reason the store kept our business was that the builder got a steep discount."

"Remember that our goal here isn't to pigeonhole people," the facilitator added. "Our only goal is to figure out how to sell to people in a way that works better for them. We use buying styles as a vehicle for improving the communication."

Manipulation?

"But isn't this manipulation?" The question came from the recruiter on the Blue Team.

"Manipulation?" the facilitator asked. "That's a fair question, of course. But help us to understand it a little better. How might it be manipulation?"

The recruiter responded. "You are just adjusting your style in order to get someone to buy from you. Isn't that manipulation?"

"If that's true," Connie said, "then, according to your definition, any sales activity is manipulation because everything we are doing is to get someone to buy from us. That would mean that writing a proposal is manipulation."

Dave could hear Connie's high-C coming to the fore.

"You know what I mean," the recruiter said. "It just doesn't seem right that we would be using these clever psychological techniques to get our way."

The facilitator stepped back in. "For this buying style information to be most useful to us, we have to be comfortable using it. And, for some of us, if we feel we are manipulating people, we may not feel good about using the tool.

"Let's consider a different perspective. My wife's stepfather is a little hard of hearing. So if I want him to hear me, I have to speak louder. Do I speak louder to manipulate him? No, I speak louder so that he can hear me. Speaking louder is the *vehicle* I use to help him hear me. Now, if my *intention* is to manipulate him, I can use speaking louder as a *vehicle* for manipulation.

"In the same way, if I want to sell to a high-D, I need her to hear me. So I will adjust my selling style so that I am prepared, brief, and then gone. This is the *vehicle* I am using so she can hear me. Now, if the product I am selling is not in her best interest and my *intention* is to sell the product anyway, then I might be using the *vehicle* for manipulation.

> *Our only goal is to figure out how to sell to people in a way that works better for them.*

"My point is that buying styles, like speaking louder, is a vehicle to help people hear you. Whether this vehicle is used for manipulation depends on your intention. Does that help?"

The recruiter responded. "I like the way you put that. The information about buying styles is just a vehicle to help people hear us better. Manipulation is determined by our intention and how we use the vehicle. So how do we make sure salespeople's intentions are pure and in the best interest of the customer?"

"Another interesting question," the facilitator said. "But that's beyond the scope of this particular morning."

"Just kidding," responded the recruiter. "We can't solve purity of motives or world hunger today. Tomorrow maybe."

"I would like for you now to look back at your list of three prospects," the facilitator said. "On the basis of the additional information we discussed, think about each of them and make adjustments to your style guesses."

Dave looked back at his list of active prospects. This additional information about recognizing the styles confirmed his guesses:

Client	Key Buyer	Status	Style	The Signs
Financial Compliance Advisers	Geoffrey Wilson, Chief Executive Officer	Active	C	• Seemed difficult to engage in casual conversation • Made three requests for revisions to our meeting agenda • Became overly agitated when the meal he ordered was not prepared to his specifications • Kept office cluttered with stacks of paper but could always access information he needed
Regent Imaging Corporation	Ross Studebaker, Chief Operating Officer	Active	D	• All meetings short and to the point • Pushed us down to work with lower people in his organization • When named head of the project midway through, did not review any of the previous documentation • Had awards on display

(continued)

Client	Key Buyer	Status	Style	The Signs
Premier Granite and Tile	John Eric, Vice President of Operations	Active	C	• Insisted on having information sent to him and then requested additional information before agreeing to a meeting • Had read all the literature and was prepared with a detailed list of questions when we first met • Had an immaculate office; never had anything on the desk

Dave was pleased that the facilitator had taken time to lay a solid foundation for understanding styles and how to recognize them. But he was eager to learn more about how to sell to the different styles.

. . . .

CHAPTER 6

Comparing Selling Styles
and Buying Styles

. . . .

"So far this morning, we have talked about the four different buying styles and how to identify them," the facilitator said. "Now we're going to talk about the four different selling styles. But I would like to cover this segment a little differently. During the next 30 minutes, rather than my doing the teaching, I want you to do it. I would like for you to describe the characteristics of each of the selling styles. What would be the natural selling tendencies of high-Ds? What would be their natural approach to selling? What would be their natural strengths and natural weaknesses? How about a high-I as a salesperson? Or a high-S or a high-C? To accomplish this, I have assigned each team to one of the styles. Red Team, you have the high-S. Green Team, take the high-D. Blue Team, you have the high-C, and, Black Team, take the high-I.

"On the flip charts that I have placed near each team's table, you have three columns: approach, strengths, and weaknesses. For the style assigned to you, answer the three questions shown."

The Questions

- What would be the natural selling approach of the style?
- What are the strengths of the selling approach?
- What are the weaknesses of the selling approach?

The facilitator continued. "High-Cs, I'm not looking for a thesis here. But high-Ds, more than one answer per column would be helpful. In fact, let's set a goal of two to four bullets per column. This is a six-minute exercise. Appoint a new team leader once more. Any questions?"

"It looks like it's my turn to lead," Dave said. "So let's talk about the high-S selling approach. How would a high-S naturally want to sell to someone?"

There were a few moments of awkward silence. Dave watched the dynamic unfold. Douglas, who would normally speak up, seemed to be deliberately trying not to behave like a high-D. Connie began turning back to earlier pages in the course manual, perhaps seeking a foundation to support what she was planning to say. Ian clearly wanted to say something—his high-I being hard to contain—but he was looking over at Sam, the team's only high-S, perhaps hoping that Sam would take the reins. Yet, Sam seemed quite content with the silence.

Finally, when Ian couldn't stand it any longer, he broke the silence. "I've had a few high-S salespeople work for me in our car dealership. I didn't know they were high-Ss at the time. But now I can understand them a lot better. The two salespeople I'm thinking of took a warm, friendly approach when selling to their customers. They would listen for as long as the customer wanted to talk. People just liked them. They weren't the most aggressive salespeople in the world, so they did not necessarily set the world on fire with their quota performance, but I'll tell you one thing: The customers they did get were very loyal. They would come back every two or three years and want to know where John or Betty was. They would want to deal only with their salesperson."

"Sounds like their loyal customers were also high-Ss. Takes one to love one," said Douglas, laughing to himself, though no one else found it amusing.

Ian responded. "That's an interesting point, Douglas. I hadn't thought about that, but you are probably correct. Their loyal customers were probably high-Ss themselves."

"Okay. So here is what I have so far," Dave said and proceeded to recap the information on his chart:

High-S Selling Style

Approach	Strengths	Weaknesses
• Warm, friendly	• Listens to customers	• Not very aggressive
	• Likable	
	• Gains loyalty of customers	

Then Sam spoke up. "I think another of our weaknesses is that we find it hard sometimes to cut off customers who are taking far more time than their current or potential level of spending would normally dictate as prudent. I have two customers that each take about four or five hours of my time a month. Yet, they are not today and probably won't ever be among my top 25 customers. But they call all the time and want to see me on a regular basis, so I show up."

Dave, noticing they were still short a point or two in the approach column, redirected Sam with a question. "So how would you describe the approach a high-S might take with customers?"

"I think warm and friendly ring true to me. I also think the words 'personable' and 'consultative' may be appropriate, as well. We want to be helpful and stay on good terms with you, so we want you to buy something that meets your needs. Because of this, I think high-Ss may have the tendency to take much more of a consultative approach to selling, rather than a pure hard-sell approach."

"Thanks, Sam," Dave said. "That was helpful."

When everyone laughed, Dave wondered why, until he reflected on how he had just praised a high-S in the way high-Ss most like to be praised.

"Time's up," said the facilitator. "The teams have given us a starting point by recording preliminary thoughts on a flip chart about the style assigned to them. I would now like to give each team a chance to rotate around, view the work of the other teams, and add to it or recommend changes to things with which you disagree. This will give people a chance to gain a much more in-depth understanding of what each of the teams has written. Red Team, please take your marker and go to the chart created by the Green Team. Green Team, go to the Blue Team's chart. Blue Team, go to the Black Team's chart. And Black Team, go to the Red Team's chart.

"Now that you are at the other team's chart, read each bullet point. If your team likes the idea, put a check mark on it. If you disagree, put an X on it and write a note for the team explaining how to fix the point and tape the note next to it. If you believe a bullet point needs to be added, write it up using your marker and place a check mark on it. When you are done, every item on that team's chart should have either a check mark or an X-mark from your team. And every X-mark should have a note right beside it explaining how to fix the point. You have four minutes. After the four minutes is up, you will rotate to the next team's chart. We will do these rotations until you get back to your own chart. Any questions?"

Dave was expecting to have a chance to present his team's work to the other tables, so he was disappointed by the "rotating flip chart" process that the facilitator described. "I wonder why we are doing the review this way," Dave said to Ian as they moved to the Green Team's flip chart.

Overhearing the conversation, Connie offered a thought. "If you think about it, the facilitator has had us doing a lot of different things today. Sometimes it's been great for the high-Ds— that darn clock the facilitator uses gets on my nerves, but I bet the high-Ds love it."

"Darn straight," Douglas responded.

"And some of the discussions are as a full group—something you Is probably like. I and possibly the other high-Cs in the room have liked it when the facilitator has given us time to write things down individually before talking about them in small groups. And I bet the high-Ss like the small group because it is more personal."

"Okay, so what's the point of this rotating flip chart thing?" asked Dave.

"He said something about giving us an opportunity to get a more in-depth understanding," Connie replied. "But why not ask him when we finish this exercise?"

Douglas intervened. "Well, if you all are finishing psychoanalyzing the class—or even if you aren't—can we get to work? We're down to a couple of minutes."

By the time Dave and his team had rotated through all the other flip charts and returned back to view their own, his question regarding the exercise had answered itself. Each time the Red Team got to a new chart, Dave could see the thinking of the original team and how the different teams (represented by different pen colors) had added items and recommended changes to the various bullet points. He could also see how, once he and his team got back to their own chart, they could revise their thinking on the basis of the input from others. Once all teams had made adjustments based on the feedback received, the four charts showed the following information:

High-D Selling Style

Approach	Strengths	Weaknesses
• Direct and to the point • Aggressive in pursuit of opportunities • Seeks to close early	• Competitive, seeks to win • Doesn't waste time on dead ends • Doesn't mind cold-calling	• Direct style may be offensive to some • Lacks warmth and friendliness • May not take time to develop leads with long-term potential

High-I Selling Style

Approach	Strengths	Weaknesses
• Seeks to build relationships • Seeks to understand hot-button issues and then use persuasion to sell	• Gregarious and friendly • Presents ideas well, can be very convincing	• Can say a lot without saying much • May not be good at follow-through • Can waste a lot of time in unproductive activities

High-S Selling Style

Approach	Strengths	Weaknesses
• Warm, friendly • Personable • Consultative, seeks to be helpful	• Listens to customers • Likable; customers want to help them succeed • Gains loyalty of customers	• Not very aggressive • Won't cut off unproductive customers • Doesn't ask for the business

High-C Selling Style

Approach	Strengths	Weaknesses
• Uses product knowledge to build case for why customers should buy • Demonstrates reliability by following through on client requests	• Good at analyzing territory • Will have done the research before calling on a client • Meticulous with follow-up	• Tends to over-prepare for sales calls • May not be friendly and warm • Can have the right product but not be able to convince the customer

From reviewing the charts, Dave could easily see how some members of his sales team strongly resembled the various selling styles. The description of the high-I captured his selling style well, even though another team prepared the information. But there was more to learn as the facilitator brought them back.

"Now that we're clear on the selling approach and strengths and weaknesses of each of the styles, we're ready to take this analysis a little further," the facilitator said.

"Let's examine each selling style and determine how individuals with each of the four buying styles would respond to that selling style. For each selling style, we'll identify which styles would probably like the selling style and which styles would probably strongly dislike the selling style. Let's start with high-D. Green Team, you had the high-D selling style, and, after the rotating review, the flip chart indicates that the high-D selling style is direct and aggressive and closes early. Think about how the various buying styles would respond to this approach. Perhaps some would find it appealing. Others might be strongly turned off by it. First, which style or styles would find it appealing?"

A member of the Green Team spoke up. "Surely the high-Ds would like that approach because that is how they communicate."

"That makes sense," said the facilitator. "Would any other style find this approach appealing?" When no one responded, the facilitator continued. "Okay, which style or styles would strongly dislike this selling style?"

"Well, I think I'm a high-C," said the same person from the Green Team, "and I find high-Ds to be pushy and overbearing. They try to force me to make a decision before giving me all the information I need."

"Let's put a check box on the high-Cs," the facilitator said. "Are there any other styles that would strongly dislike the high-D selling style?"

"I would bet the high-Ss wouldn't like the selling style, either," said Ian. "They might see the aggressive style as unfriendly and too businesslike." Ian looked over at Sam, who nodded his agreement.

"So, to recap," the facilitator said, "we believe high-Ds would resonate to the high-D selling style, but high-Ss and high-Cs would strongly dislike the style. Let's go on to the next selling style, the high-I."

Once the facilitator had led the group through all four selling styles, he had created a chart with the following information:

Selling Style		How would the style react? Like (L) Strongly Dislike (D)			
		D	I	S	C
High-D	Is direct and aggressive, closes early	L		D	D
High-I	Is gregarious, persuasive		L	L	D
High-S	Is personable, consultative	D	L	L	
High-C	Is thorough, knowledgeable, reliable	D	D		L

"Please keep in mind," the facilitator warned, "that we are talking about dominant selling styles here. As you will see when you get your individual selling style report, most of us are high in more than one of the four styles. However, at any given time, one of these styles dominates our sales approach. Yet, if someone naturally sells with the high-D style, he or she can still adjust when selling to another style, such as a high-S or a high-C. The point is to be conscious of your natural tendencies and to adjust your selling style when appropriate."

"So, when is it appropriate to adjust your selling style?" Douglas asked.

"Good question. Judging from the chart we just created, it is appropriate most often—but not in all cases—when you are selling to a style different from your own. For high-Ds, when they are selling to high-Ss and high-Cs, the chart suggests they would do well to adapt. When high-Is are selling to high-Cs, when high-Ss are selling to high-Ds, and when high-Cs are selling to high-Ds and high-Is, adapting could prove to be very helpful."

"Before we go further," said the facilitator, "I would like for us to test the table you all have created. I want to ask that question: Have we been more successful when selling to styles that like our selling style, and do we lose more often when we sell to styles that dislike our selling style? Intuitively, you might expect the answer to be yes. But let's check it, using the list of clients you brought with you and completing the chart in your books, which I have displayed on the screen.

A Style Comparison of Your Wins and Losses

	Wins		Losses	
Your Style	Like	Dislike	Like	Dislike

"First, identify what you think your natural style is, and write that into the chart. Next, review each of your wins and the style you identified for the client. On the basis of the selling styles table we've created, does that client's style like your selling style or dislike it, or is it neutral to your selling style? Count the number of the wins that 'like' your selling style according to the table and the number of wins that 'dislike' your selling style. If you are a high-D and two of your wins are with high-Ds and one is with a high-S, you would place a 2 in the Wins-Like column and 1 in the Wins-Dislike column. Then do the same thing with your three losses, identifying the number of likes and dislikes. Do that individually first. Then, team leaders, get the numbers from each of your team members and tally them to get the numbers for your table. When you are done, bring the tally for your table to the front of the room."

Dave reviewed his list and was quickly able to summarize his results:

Dave's Client List

Client	Key Buyer	Status	Style
Fasteners in a Snap	Jillian McFarland, Vice President of Administration	Win	S
Better Beverage Makers	Bob Scott, Chief Executive Officer	Win	I
Ebank Finances	Vance Paulson, Director of European Expansion Unit	Win	I

(continued)

Client	Key Buyer	Status	Style
Web Systems and Tools	Sharlene Case, Vice President of Administration and Technology	Loss	C
Global Tech Electronic Specialists	Myron Griffin, Senior Vice President	Loss	C
The Candy Company	Fiona Young, Vice President of Sales	Loss	D

Dave's Summary

	Wins		Losses	
Your Style	Like	Dislike	Like	Dislike
High-I	3	0	0	2

Five minutes later, the results from the four teams were tallied on a chart at the front of the room and totaled. Given that there were 20 participants in the class, each with three wins and three losses, the results were based on 60 wins and 60 losses.

Dave expected the results to be favorable when the selling style matched the buyer's style, but he was not prepared for how skewed the results would be:

	Wins		Losses	
Team	Like	Dislike	Like	Dislike
Red	11	2	4	8

	Wins		Losses	
Team	Like	Dislike	Like	Dislike
Green	13	1	5	8
Blue	11	3	2	10
Black	9	3	3	9
Total	44	9	14	35
Percentage out of 60 wins/losses	73%	15%	23%	58%

Without offering any conclusions himself, the facilitator invited the group to comment on the data in the chart. It was Connie who spoke first.

"This is intriguing information. If I'm reading the data correctly—and admittedly we don't have anything close to an unbiased sample—these percentages indicate that we had nearly a five times greater likelihood of winning when our natural selling style was compatible with the client's style than when the styles weren't compatible (73 percent versus 15 percent). And we were more than 2.5 times more likely to lose when our selling style wasn't compatible with our client's buying style (23 percent versus 58 percent)."

"Do you usually see such dramatic results in a class like this?" Dave asked.

"Let's just say that the results are not atypical," the facilitator responded.

"So does this mean that we as sales managers should do a

better job of matching our salespeople with our customers?" Dave continued.

"Wait a minute," said the clothing store sales manager. "I don't want to be bothered with making sure we have multiple D, I, S, and C salespeople on the floor at all times. Isn't it better to teach our salespeople how to adapt their selling styles to match the style of the customer?"

"Clearly, that's the better answer," Dave said, as he could see the many heads nodding in agreement around the room.

. . . .

CHAPTER 7

Tailoring Your Sales Approach to Your Customer's Buying Style

. . . .

"It looks like we are in agreement that it is better to teach salespeople how to adapt to the buying style of the customer," the facilitator said. "So now it is time to talk about how to tailor your sales approach to each of the specific styles. The goal is for us to learn how to sell to each customer in the way he or she wants to be sold."

Tailoring to a High-D
. . . .

"Let's start with the high-D," the facilitator continued. "Let's say that you sell insurance and are meeting with a person who exhibits behaviors that suggest he is a high-D. What might those behaviors be?"

"High-Ds are my favorite type," said the saleswoman from the computer hardware manufacturer. "They are decisive, they know what they want, and they expect you to be prepared and get straight to the point."

"So if that is their attitude, tell me more about their behaviors," the facilitator said. "Think about the things that high-Ds do that let you know they are decisive or that they want you to get straight to the point. What behaviors would you expect from high-Ds when talking with them about insurance that would let you know their buying style?"

The saleswoman responded, "Okay, I get what you're asking. One of the things that they do is look you straight in the eye. They also take control of the conversation and make you get down to business right away. They'll say something like, 'Tell me what you can do for me.' And if you start going into too much detail, they will stop you in your tracks."

"With that said, if you conclude that this customer is a high-D," the facilitator added, "keep in mind that she wants you to get to the point, so give her the bottom line and let her control the conversation. High-Ds will tune out if you take too long to get to the point."

The facilitator put up a chart and indicated, "Here are key tips for tailoring your approach for high-Ds."

High-D Tailoring Tips

In general . . .	• Let them control the conversation.
	• State your points directly and concisely.
	• Focus on the benefit to be achieved.
	• Close by asking for the business.

Avoid . . .

- Wasting their time with information, details, or activities that they may consider unnecessary.

To start . . .

- Be direct; put the high-D in control (*"What can I do for you?"*).

When conversing . . .

- Let the high-D control the flow of the conversation.
- Be clear and concise with your questions and direct with your responses.

When presenting . . .

- Give the recommendation first followed by the problem it solves, and the benefits to be achieved.
- Use visual displays and graphs to clarify points.

When writing . . .

- Be as brief as possible.
- Use bullet points.
- Provide one-page summaries.

When asking for a decision . . .

- Don't offer many alternatives; high-Ds want your best recommendation and need to know only that you have considered the many options for them.
- Stress the impact of your proposal and how it will bring tangible results.

They will tune out if . . .

- You take too long to get to the point.

To regain their attention . . .   ● *"Let me get straight to the point."*

     ● *"Suppose I skip the details and just hit the highlights?"*

In summary . . .   ● Be prepared, be brief, be gone.

Tailoring to a High-I

"Next is the high-I. Let's take a different example. Let's say you sell training classes and have just reached by phone the head of training for a corporation to whom you have been trying to sell for several months. Within the first minute of your phone call, you conclude she is a high-I. What signs might indicate the person is a high-I?"

The recruiter from the Blue Team responded first. "That's a common situation for me. I work with VPs of HR, and they are often high-Is. I think the telltale signs in the first minute of a phone call are the person's energy level and responsiveness."

"How do you mean?" asked the facilitator.

"I know exactly what he means," said Ian, jumping into the conversation. "High-Is tend to sound kind of perky—and they talk with you like you're a long lost friend, even over the phone. When I sold in our fleet department, I called on corporate fleet managers all the time. I could easily tell the high-Is."

"That's exactly what I mean," said the recruiter. "It's almost like they are waiting for someone to come along to talk with. And, boy, do they talk! I had one high-I on the phone the other day, And he practically told me his whole life story. He was from. . ."

"Whoa," the facilitator interrupted. "Let me redirect this conversation a bit back to tailoring."

"Right. Sorry about that," Ian said. "I guess you have to keep us high-Is in line."

"Okay, so we have talked about how you can quickly recognize a high-I over the phone," said the facilitator. "Now let's talk about how to tailor your selling style to match their buying style."

The chart that the facilitator put up indicated the following information:

High-I Tailoring Tips

In general . . .	• Be warm, friendly, and upbeat.
	• Start with the big picture ideas first.
	• Give them plenty of time to talk.
Avoid . . .	• Diving straight into business.
	• Focusing on details.
	• Telling versus asking.
To start . . .	• Be warm, friendly, and upbeat (*"Hi! I'm . . . welcome to our store."*).
When conversing . . .	• Let them take their time getting to the point.
	• When making a point, ask for their feedback; give them a chance to share their ideas.
	• Stress uniqueness; they respond to new or out-of-the-ordinary ideas.

When presenting . . .	• Allow time for people to network by planning a gathering time in the agenda.
	• Give them the big picture before going into details.
	• Provide them an opportunity to share their ideas before presenting your own.
	• When sharing your ideas, provide them a picture of the future.
	• Focus them on your ideas by asking them to give the benefit of your idea.
When writing . . .	• Start warm and friendly ("*I hope you had a great weekend!*").
	• Describe the overall purpose of your correspondence.
	• Invite their input.
	• Propose a meeting.
	(Avoid writing if you can; high-Is prefer to interact face-to-face.)
When asking for a decision . . .	• Dream with them by describing a vision of the possibilities and the result their decision will create.
	• Be conceptual; relate to a broader concept or idea.
	• Provide high-level information, not specific detail.
They will tune out if . . .	• You focus on facts and figures or don't make the conversation interactive.

To regain their attention . . .	• *"I would like to get your thoughts on . . ."*
	• *"Brainstorm with me how to . . ."*
	• *"Let's save the details for later."*
In summary . . .	• Let them sell themselves.

Tailoring to a High-S

"We've talked about the high-D and high-I. Let's move on to the high-S," said the facilitator. "Let's say you sell computer software that ensures that all the computers in an organization are kept up-to-date with the latest software. For the past three weeks you have been calling on a company's chief information officer, or CIO, to arrange an appointment but have been unsuccessful getting her on the phone. Then, from out of the blue, you get a call from her executive assistant letting you know that the CIO has agreed to meet with you. When you meet with the CIO in her office, within two minutes you conclude she is probably a high-S.

"I'm going to ask you to work in teams to identify some of the signs that would make it clear this person was a high-S. Select a team leader, and then take three minutes to think about what she may have said or done in those first two minutes that would communicate to you that she was a high-S. What might some of those signs be? Record each sign on a separate sheet."

Once the teams completed their work, the facilitator said, "Now let's build a list of unique answers, starting this time with the Black Team. Black Team, give me your best answer as to how we would recognize within two minutes that the CIO was a high-S."

"One of the clear signs that we've discussed before is that there would likely be family pictures in her office," the sports agent from the Black Team responded.

"Okay, got that one," said the facilitator. "Red Team, your best one?"

Sam spoke for the Red Team. "She would likely be warm but a bit reserved early in the conversation."

"Warm, but reserved," said the facilitator as he wrote. "Green Team?"

"She would show an interest in getting to know you," the government lobbyist responded.

"Explain that one, if you would. How would she do that?" the facilitator asked.

"It's like when I meet with congressional representatives to talk about important legislation that can affect one of my clients," said the lobbyist. "There are some who actually ask questions about me, my background, how much I enjoy my job, and so on. They know I'm a lobbyist and am there to advocate a position. But they tend to treat me like a human being. The Cs just want to spend the entire time focused on the issue, and the Ds seem to want to get me out of there as quickly as possible. And then there are the Is. I have to work doubly hard to get them to stop talking so that they can hear what I have to say. I have always tried to adapt to the person with whom I was speaking. But, now that I understand buying styles, it will be much easier for me to recognize the styles and know what I have to do."

"Thanks for the explanation," the facilitator said. "What about the Blue Team?"

"We had a lot of trouble with this one," said the environmental controls distributor from the Blue Team. "We also indicated the ones about family pictures and warmth mentioned by the Red and Green Teams. But then we went dry. We couldn't come up with anything else. In fact, we spent the rest of the time talking about what we wouldn't see."

"The point you are making is very insightful," the facilitator said. "Since high-Ss tend to be flexible and accommodating, they are often more easily recognized by what they are not doing. So give us a few examples of what your team said high-Ss would not do."

"We said that high-Ss wouldn't be demanding or pushy," began the environmental controls distributor. "They wouldn't try to control the conversation. They wouldn't be overly talkative. They wouldn't be super-detail-oriented. They would basically let you do your thing."

Dave understood why Sam was smiling at this last comment.

"Okay, now that we have talked about how you would recognize a high-S," said the facilitator, "let's move on to how you would tailor your sales approach to the high-S. Remember that with high-Ss the key is keeping the atmosphere friendly and warm." The facilitator reviewed the following chart with the participants.

High-S Tailoring Tips

In general . . .	• Keep the atmosphere friendly and warm.
	• Provide assurances that your solution will work.
	• Stress the positive impact on people.

Avoid . . .	* Starting with business.
	* Being pushy or discourteous.
	* Asking questions that put them on the spot.
	* Assuming that they agree with you.
To start . . .	* Be personable; let them know you are wanting to help (*"Hi! I'm . . . how can I help you today?"*).
When conversing. . .	* Show an interest in them and their needs (*"What are the most important things to you in making this purchase? Will that help you by . . . ?"*).
	* Make it easy for them to say yes or no (*"I'd love to hear what you like about this, as well as any concerns you have about it working."*).
When presenting . . .	* Allow time for people to connect with one another.
	* Present ideas deliberately and clearly.
	* Stress the positive impact on people.
	* Show how the idea has worked well in the past.
When writing . . .	* Start with a personal connection (*"I hope your weekend was great."*).
	* State your ideas as suggestions that have benefited others (*"You may find it helpful to do*

something like what customer XYZ did. They . . .").

- Suggest meeting or holding a telephone conversation.

(Avoid writing if you can; high-Ss prefer to interact face-to-face or to have a telephone conversation.)

When asking for a decision . . .
- Focus on how their decision will positively impact others *(By you doing this, your people will appreciate that they will be able to . . .).*

They will tune out if . . .
- You become pushy, demanding, or forceful.

To regain their attention . . .
- *"What's really important here is to make sure you are completely comfortable and you make the decision that you deem best for your people."*

- *"Is this a good time to recap what you are comfortable with and what is not quite comfortable yet?"*

In summary . . .
- Start personal; don't assume.

Tailoring to a High-C

"We've covered the high-D, high-I, and high-S," said the facilitator. "That leaves the high-C. Let's start with the Black Team with this question. Presume that you are a salesperson working in the new car sales department of a local car dealership. You are in the showroom when you notice someone drive up, get out of his car, and begin looking at various vehicles you have on the lot. What are the behaviors that will alert you that this person might be a high-C?"

The real estate agent began first. "We don't get this type a lot in the real estate market, but when they show up, you know it. They always have all these pages of paper. Usually it is Internet research that they have done or brochures from houses they have already seen that they want to use for comparison purposes. Sometimes the papers are in a folder. Other times they are on a clipboard. I had one woman walk in with a three-ring notebook with color-coded tabs, with each tab representing a neighborhood she was considering. It was quite impressive, really."

"Why do you think she did that?" asked the facilitator.

"I suppose she wanted everything organized so that she could be more confident that she had the information she needed when it was time to make the decision," the real estate agent said.

"So high-Cs are often readily apparent because they exhibit the signs that say 'Help me be confident I am making the right decision,'" said the facilitator. "What other ways might we recognize a high-C?"

The fundraiser from the Blue Team weighed in. "Well, another thing that they do is ask a lot of questions and take a lot of notes. Sometimes they ask the same question two or three different ways. I used to find this particularly irritating."

"I suspect there may be others in the room who still find this habit of high-Cs a bit irritating," the facilitator said. "Can you elaborate a little? Would you mind giving us a little insight into why this used to irritate you and why it doesn't anymore?"

"Well," the fundraiser responded, "I guess it irritated me when they did this because I thought they were asking the same question just to see if I would give the same answer each time—sort of like a police interrogation tactic. But, after getting to know one of our high-C donors pretty well, I now understand that this is just their way of gaining clarity and making sure the answer you give fits in all cases."

"With that said, let's get into how to tailor your sales approach to high-Cs," said the facilitator.

Ian turned to Dave and whispered, "I guess this is the part you've been waiting for, huh?"

Dave listened intently as the facilitator walked through the charts:

High-C Tailoring Tips

In general . . .	• Present ideas in a logical, linear, step-by-step manner.
	• Provide the details needed and give time to get comfortable with them.
	• Include alternatives; outline pros and cons of each.
	• Provide supporting evidence to back up claims.
	• Do what you say you are going to do.
Avoid . . .	• Being disorganized or making random comments.

- Making statements that you can't prove.
- Trying to use emotion to convince.
- Forcing a rapid decision.

To start . . .
- Send information ahead of time if possible.
- *"I have several approaches for you to look at. Let's walk through this step-by-step."*

When conversing . . .
- Stay on topic.
- Take your time; provide a sense of unhurriedness.
- Offer to walk through supporting data.

When presenting . . .
- Present in chronological order or use a structured flow such as finding, conclusion, recommendation, benefit.
- Be precise; use ranges and probabilities when precise information is not available.

When writing . . .
- Get straight to the point.
- Have a clear, logical flow.
- Provide options.
- End by suggesting a deadline for a decision.

When asking for a decision . . .
- Provide options with strengths and weaknesses for each.

They will tune out if . . .	• You make claims without providing evidence or try to force a rapid decision.
To regain their attention . . .	• *"Let's not rush into something unnecessarily."*
	• *"Let's identify what we know and where we need more information."*
In summary . . .	• Give them time for the details.

When the facilitator finished, Douglas's hand went up. Once acknowledged, he said, "Your points make sense to me. And I can see how a salesperson would likely be more successful if he or she took this approach with a high-C."

When Douglas paused to find the right words, the facilitator said, "I think I hear a 'but' coming."

"Exactly," Douglas said. "But I'm just not sure I can do this. I'm not even sure I *want* to do this. We are salespeople. We are spontaneous. I'm afraid if I have to spend a lot of time thinking about what the style of the other person is and how I should tailor to that person, I'll lose my edge, I won't be in the moment, I won't be confident, and I'll lose the sale because I'm overthinking things."

"Douglas is making a valid point," said the facilitator. "We can possibly lose sales by trying to overthink a situation. Who wants to respond?"

Adapt or continue to be so much less successful than you could be.

The response came from an unexpected source. "It would be great for you if all of your prospects were high-Ds," said Dave. "And it would be great for me if all of mine were high-Is. And perhaps Connie with her accounting business wishes all her prospects were high-Cs. But that's not the way things play out. So the message is really quite simple. Adapt or continue to be so much less successful than you could be. When I think back to all the sales we as a class reported losing when selling to prospects whose buying style didn't match our selling style, it's frightening. But, of course, we can ignore all this if we want. As the motivational speaker Les Brown puts it, 'You want to keep on gettin' what you gettin'? Just keep on doin' what you doin'.' I'm going to try this because I don't want to keep gettin' what I'm gettin'."

"I look at it a little differently," Ian added. "I played singles tennis for many years before I began playing doubles. And, when you play doubles, you have to learn a new set of instincts. How you move in the court, the timing for when you rush the net, when you play back, when to lob, when to cross-court—it's different with doubles. In the beginning, it felt unnatural, and I had to talk myself through just about every point. After a while, though, it became instinctive. I knew where to be and what to do. And, in fact, playing doubles has improved my singles game. I think this will be the same way. Applying this information will feel awkward at first. It certainly will feel awkward for me in trying to adapt to high-Cs. But, over time, as it becomes more instinctive, I expect it will help me both with the styles I find difficult as well as the styles I find easy."

CHAPTER 8

Recognizing Style Clashes

· ·

"Let's shift over now," the facilitator told the group. "We have been talking about how to tailor your selling style to your customer's buying style. Now focus on style clashes: What are they, why do they occur, how do we recognize them, and what can we do about them? Let's start by recalling the dimensions graph from earlier today.

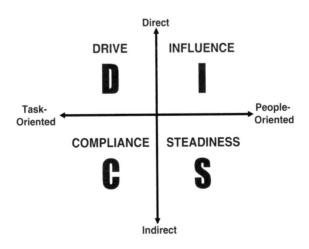

"I have a question and I want to direct it to the Green Team. According to the chart, high-Is tend to be direct and people-oriented. Which of the selling styles would likely have the greatest problem with high-Is?"

"Probably the high-Cs because they are indirect and task-oriented," the government lobbyist responded.

"That's correct," said the facilitator. "Now let's take this further. What would the high-Cs say about the high-Is? What would be their biggest complaint?"

The retail store sales manager jumped in first. "I hear it all the time from my operations people. They say we sales folks just talk a good game, never follow through, don't get anything in on time, and are always shoddy about the details. And they're right!"

"Sounds like your operations people have your team pegged," the facilitator said. "So let's reverse the question. What would the high-Is say about the high-Cs? What would be their biggest complaint?"

"They would probably say that high-Cs are anal to a fault, are real killjoys when it comes to discussing ideas, and probably couldn't sell their way out of a paper bag," the pharmaceutical salesperson responded.

Connie didn't miss a beat when she quipped, "To which us high-Cs say, 'Thank you so much for the compliment!'"

"So, if you think about it," said the facilitator, "what do high-Is need? Someone to rein them in and give their ideas substance, something high-Cs happen to be very good at. And what do high-Cs need? Someone with ideas, creativity, and a sense of fun. Again, a great job description for a high-I. In essence, the high-I/high-C partnership is a match made in heaven, or the other place, depending upon whether each learns to value the other's style.

"Blue Team, let's do the same with the other diagonal. A high-S is indirect and people-oriented. So, of course, the selling style that is least like the high-S is the high-D, which is direct and task-oriented. So, Blue Team, what would the high-Ss say about the high-Ds? What would be their biggest complaint?"

"High-Ss would say that the high-Ds are aggressive to the point of being pushy and demanding and too focused on profits and not people," the nonprofit fundraiser responded.

"I guess it is my turn to say thank you," Douglas said.

"And, Blue Team, what would the high-Ds say about the high-Ss?" asked the facilitator.

A distributor for an environmental controls company said, "I would bet that high-Ds would consider the high-Ss too soft on people. They probably would complain that the high-Ss don't speak up a lot of the time and don't seem willing to step up and address the tough issues."

Ian jumped in. "It may be that they don't want to rock the boat if there is no reason to."

"All good points," the facilitator said. "Keep in mind, however, that, like the high-I/high-C combination, the high-D/high-S can be a partnership made in heaven or the other place, depending upon whether each learns to value the other's style. What do high-Ds need? People to follow them. What do high-Ss desire? A good king or a cause they can believe in and support.

"Yes, the styles are different. But, by valuing the strengths of the other styles and by communicating with them in a way that is more effective, we can increase the effectiveness of the relationship and can greatly enhance our sales productivity. They buy from us because we understand them, speak their language, and sell to them in the way they want to buy.

"So, at this point, we have talked about the classic style clashes. Let me tie this back to a discussion we had earlier. Recall that, at the start of the day, we built a list of behaviors we find most challenging. You may remember that I said that, through the list, you told me more about yourselves than you told me about your customers. Let me show you what I meant. Let's start with the Red Team's list."

The facilitator continued. "The first item says, 'They waste your time and then do nothing.' Red Team, which style tends to exhibit that behavior?"

Behaviors We Hate from Customers: The Red Team's List

- They waste your time and then do nothing.
- The buyer sends you to purchasing.
- They aren't clear what they want, and they change things.
- They don't return your phone calls.
- They want to tell you their life story.

Ian recognized his comment and said, "High-C definitely. They waste your time having you test-drive all the different cars with them. They want you to gather all the fact sheets for every car they look at. They analyze information from the consumer magazines. They meet with you four or five times. Then, in the end, they do nothing!"

"So, Ian," the facilitator asked, "if the behavior you find most challenging in people is a high-C behavior, more than likely what is your dominant style?"

Dave could see the revelation come over Ian's face. "Okay, I get it," Ian said. "If I'm having trouble with high-Cs, more than likely it is because my style is just the opposite, a high-I."

"It doesn't always work that way, but, more times than not, it is indeed the case," said the facilitator. "And that makes sense, doesn't it? The behaviors you hate from your customers are often the reverse of your own selling style. But let's look at the other comments and figure out which style each represents, as well as the likely style of the person who made the comment—though we don't have to name names!"

When the group was done with the Red Team, the facilitator had created the following chart:

Behaviors We Hate—The Red Team's List	Customer's Likely Style	Seller's Likely Style
They waste your time and then do nothing.	C	I
The buyer sends you to purchasing.	C	I
They aren't clear what they want, and they change things.	I	C
They don't return your phone calls.	D	S
They want to tell you their life story.	S	D

....

The behaviors you hate from your
customers are often the reverse
of your own selling style.

....

"On the basis of this information," the facilitator continued, "you have probably figured out that another approach to determining the buying style of others is to ask them, 'When it comes to working with a salesperson, what are the behaviors that drive you nuts?' Then you listen closely to their response and determine the style that the behavior represents. The person's buying style is likely the opposite."

Douglas wasn't done with his challenges. "I don't understand why you are making it so complicated. Why not just ask them how they want you to sell to them?"

"Of course, Douglas," said the facilitator, "if that works for you, then by all means do it. It is a more direct approach and may get you there quicker. What we find, though, is that when we ask people how they want to be sold to, many can't offer a well-defined answer. In essence, many don't know what they want. But, just about everyone knows what they don't want. By asking the negative question, you may find you get a quicker answer."

Connie found herself smiling again. Douglas was beginning to wear on her. Yet, even when challenged, the facilitator affirmed Douglas's position and then gave him a reason to do something else. "Well done," she said quietly to herself.

"It's time to get back to Dave's question from earlier today," the facilitator said. "What if you guess wrong? What if, with all that we have learned about recognizing buying styles, we still get it wrong and we begin selling to the customer in the wrong style? How will we know, and what do we do about it?

"Let's tackle this by reflecting on each buying style. Let's start with the high-D again, starting with Dave and going around the table. Dave, what is the key factor for a high-D?"

"Time," Dave responded.

"That's right," said the facilitator. "So, if we are abusing their key factor, what are we doing, Ian?"

"We are wasting their time," Ian said.

"Right again. So, Sam, consider this. If we are abusing their key factor, that is, when we are wasting their time, what do high-Ds do? What do they do when we are selling to them in the wrong style?"

Sam responded, "They get impatient. They look at their watch. They start multitasking so as not to waste their time."

"That's a very nice description of a high-D when we are selling to them in the wrong style," the facilitator responded. "As Sam said, they get impatient, they start doing other things. You may have thought this person was a high-C, so you were providing a review of the details. But, if you see these behaviors, they are signs that you are communicating in the wrong style.

"How do you recover? You might say something like, 'Let's see if I can summarize this for you so we can save time' or 'Let me cut to the chase here and give you the bottom line.' When they hear you adapting to their style, they will appreciate it, and it is more likely that you will get their attention."

"I like that," said Douglas, giving his sole praise for the day. "Those are great suggestions because they would definitely work on me. In fact, I want to go back and tell my direct reports that this is exactly what they should do whenever they see me checking out."

"Thanks, Douglas. So let's move on to the Green Team to answer the same questions for the high-Is."

Once they had reviewed all four of the styles, Dave looked at the summary flip chart:

	Key Factor	Your Behavior	Their Behavior	Your Response
D	Time	Wasting their time	Impatience, looking at watch, multitasking	*"Let me cut to the chase here and give you the bottom line."*
I	Being heard	Not giving them a chance to speak; being too detailed	Interrupting, checking out mentally	*"I would like to get your thoughts on . . . brainstorm with me how to . . . let's save the details for later."*
S	Being liked	Being pushy or abrasive	Shutting down, becoming passive-aggressive	*"There may be good reasons for not doing this; let's identify potential strengths and weaknesses."*
C	Getting it right	Forcing a rapid decision	Objecting, arguing, finding fault	*"Let's not rush into something unnecessarily . . . let's identify what we know and where we need more information."*

Dave found himself shaking his head. He was thinking about the recent loss to Web Systems and Tools. How many times had he misread the style of the primary buyer, Sharlene Case? During the entire sales cycle he had treated her like a high-I, giving her high-level information, trying to wine and dine her and her team. Yet, she never showed up at any of the dinners or anything else that looked like a social function. She also was the one who wanted more and more details. But Dave also thought that she had to have a high-S as well because, when she objected or found fault, it was always very nicely put and nothing Dave took seriously until he lost the bid. But what Dave was going to learn was that his selling style mistake was small by comparison to the mistake the facilitator was about to describe.

The Facilitator's Mistake

"It's always humbling, isn't it, when you make a mistake that *you teach others* not to make and it costs you dearly?" the facilitator began. "I would like to relate an experience of mine in the hope that you might avoid similar situations.

"A very large technology company requested that we bid on providing consulting training to their 2,000+ system engineers located around the globe. Our first call was with the chief recommender, the person leading the team responsible for recommending a training organization to management. We concluded that the chief recommender's buying style appeared to be a high-S/high-C. After doing our work to define the need and identify the competition, we concluded that we had two key differentiators. First, our course content is designed to help their system engineers position themselves as trusted advisers with their customers as opposed to technical contractors. And, second, our instructional methodology would keep the class practical, dynamic, and highly interactive. (We call this our PDI difference.)

"Given the style of the chief recommender, our plan for the presentation was to demonstrate the depth of our content, as well as our interactive presentation style. For a number of reasons, the two-hour presentation of our proposal to the potential client had to be done as a Webinar. We were not present in the room with the team making the decision.

"In starting the session, we used our interactive process of gathering their critical questions and matching their questions to our proposed presentation agenda. The chief recommender appeared a bit impatient during this, so I hurried it along. During the session, the chief recommender seemed to want to push the presentation in the direction of how we were going to make sure we learned about their environment. While I responded to his questions, I felt I wasn't connecting with him.

"When we moved on to giving a demonstration of one of our modules, he cut it short, and, while one of his colleagues indicated value in the content and the methods, he indicated that it was too slow and not at the right level for veteran system engineers. We agreed with him that if it were too slow or at the incorrect level, that would not be good. So, therefore, our approach included bringing together a team of their subject matter experts to assist in a full-needs assessment to ensure that we delivered the right information, at the right pace, to address their needs.

"I thought we would score big points with that comment. But the chief recommender felt this meant our lack of knowledge of their culture would require more time from them in order for us to be successful.

"After the completion of the presentation, our team debriefed and agreed on an approach to continue our sales effort. Our client relationship manager sent an e-mail that acknowledged the chief recommender's concern about our knowledge of their organization, highlighted our approach to address the concern, reminded him of the key value we brought to the table, and requested feedback.

"The chief recommender explained in his reply that he felt our training was *not* practical, *not* dynamic, *not* interactive, *not* at all engaging.

"We were, of course, stunned! We pride ourselves in PDI—and have hundreds of clients who have given us feedback over the years that our approaches are highly engaging. I wrote him an e-mail asking a question: 'What would your chief technology officer do if he learned that a potential client had concluded that your technology was not integrated, not scalable, and not adaptable—just the opposite of what hundreds of your clients would say?' I then described what I thought the chief technology officer would do and then said we are in the same situation. The e-mail was about a page in length.

"The chief recommender wrote back, 'I appreciate the spirit of this response, but to be successful with our organization you need to net out the bottom line. Your e-mail was far too long, and I didn't read it. I don't have time to try to figure out what points you were trying to make. . . . Other presenters did a better job of communicating their value and proposed solution.'

"It was only then I realized that, during this entire interaction, I had been communicating with him as if he were a high-S/high-C and not adapting to the signs of a high-D buying style! I reflected back and realized that, because I thought I already knew his buying style and was caught up in the presentation, I had not connected the dots that shouted high-D: his *impatience* as he tried to push the agenda along, his comments about the training being too *slow*, his concern about us causing him more *time* because we didn't know his organization—and I teach this stuff!

"How did I miss it? Why didn't I see the need to adapt? I suspect that his position and role in the company, our initial interaction, and my initial conclusion about his style may have prevented me from seeing what was, upon reflection, more than obvious.

"If I had responded appropriately, might we have had a different outcome? I can't say for sure. But I can say for sure that not responding to his buying style certainly nailed shut the opportunity for a multiyear, multimillion-dollar assignment.

"The only good thing about this story is that I get to share it with you. Don't let this happen to you. Pay close attention to buying styles. It can make a significant difference.

"We are about to take our second break," the facilitator told the group. "But, before we do, I will be giving you your personal style report, which is based on the survey you completed before coming to class. This report will detail your natural selling style and will provide you insights on how to adapt your style to that of others. During the break, review the report, identify any questions you have, and we'll have a question-and-answer session toward the end of the class. Let's take that break now."

CHAPTER 9

· ·

Planning Your Next Steps

· ·

D
ave was amazed at how accurately his report seemed to match him. He indeed came out as a high-I/high-S, with a very low C and a moderate D. He liked the recommended tips for dealing with the various styles and was intrigued by the discussion of his self-perception and how others perceive him when he is under moderate and extreme pressure.

But, rather than spending more time reviewing his individual report, following the break Dave focused on developing a plan for how he was going to guide his team in handling the three active accounts he had brought to the class.

"This final segment in the course is about planning your next steps," the facilitator began. "What do you do with all this information? I would like for you to take the next ten minutes to use the worksheets that follow to review your three active accounts and answer the following questions. First, what style is the principal buyer, and what evidence do you have that this is the case? Second, what approaches are you *already using* that are aligned with this person's buying style? Third, what should you *start doing* to better align with this person's buying style? Fourth, what should you *stop doing* to better align with this person's buying style? And, finally, of all the responses you give, which are the first, second, and third most important for you to implement in the next 30 days. Any questions?"

Dave was excited about the tools he had received from the class and went straight to work on his three active accounts:

Account	Financial Compliance Advisers
Key Buyer	Geoffrey Wilson, Chief Executive Officer
Which Style? **How Do You** **Know?**	High-C • Seemed difficult to engage in casual conversation • Made three requests for revisions to our meeting agenda • Became overly agitated when the meal he ordered was not prepared to his specifications • Kept office cluttered with stacks of paper but could always access information he needed

Adapting to the Buying Style

Already Doing	Arranged a demonstration
Start Doing	• Make sure our team keeps a list of his requests and follows up promptly • Remember that trust for high-Cs is earned by following through, providing details, doing the things that show they can trust my assurances
Stop Doing	• Trying to get him involved in social, relationship-building activities • Making claims without evidence

Account	Regent Imaging Corporation
Key Buyer	Ross Studebaker, Chief Operating Officer
Which Style? How Do You Know?	High-D • All meetings short and to the point • Pushed us down to work with lower people in his organization • When named head of the project midway through, did not review any of the previous documentation • Had awards on display

Adapting to the Buying Style

Already Doing	• Kept voice mail messages brief
Start Doing	• Start with the recommendation first in all e-mails, voice mails • Be specific about value; show the cost/benefit • Let him control the conversation
Stop Doing	• Trying to get him involved in social, relationship-building activities

Account	Premier Granite and Tile
Key Buyer	John Eric, Vice President of Operations
Which Style? How Do You Know?	High-C • Insisted on having information sent to him and then requested additional information before agreeing to a meeting

(continued)

Account	Premier Granite and Tile
	• Had read all the literature and was prepared with a detailed list of questions when we first met • Had an immaculate office; never had anything on the desk

Adapting to the Buying Style

Already Doing	• Provided a detailed specification manual
Start Doing	• Make sure our team keeps a list of his requests and follows up promptly • Ask, "What more can we do to provide you the detail you need to make an informed decision?" • Remember that trust for high-Cs is earned by following through, providing details, doing the things that show they can trust my assurances
Stop Doing	• Trying to get him involved in social, relationship-building activities • Making claims without evidence

Seeing his plans in black and white made it clear to Dave how he, and probably most of his team, had made a bad habit of trying to sell the same way to every client. For Dave, it was the relationship sale. And, for all three of these prospects, it was important that he not emphasize this because the approach is often not fruitful when selling to high-Ds and high-Cs.

"The clock has sounded," the facilitator said, "and it is time for us to move to the second stage of planning. You have already planned for these specific accounts. Now I would like for you to think more generally. We'll be working in our teams. So select a new team leader, and, team leaders, use the marker and pads for this, with one item per page, please. Here's the question:

"Imagine that two years from now the concept of 'Buying Styles: Simple Lessons for Selling the Way Your Customer Buys' has become an integral part of your sales culture. Think about the things that would have to happen to bring this about. Consider the things that occurred over the two years that made buying styles part of your everyday selling life. Now take four minutes to brainstorm with your team members things that *could* be done to make buying styles part of your sales culture."

"Okay, fellows," Connie said, "your high-C team member has grabbed the pen. You heard the question. What might you do to make buying styles part of your culture?"

Ian jumped right in. "This information is very helpful. I need to share this with the sales reps in the dealership. I'm thinking that a good way to keep it fresh is to have my reps, when they come to meet with me to review a customer proposal, indicate which style they think the potential customer is and how they have adjusted to that style. This would help keep the information fresh."

"For me," Sam said, "I would want to continue to use the planning sheet when working with top customers until the information became a regular way of thinking. I probably would need to review the workbook often to keep it fresh."

Dave responded next. "My company is definitely going to have to get all of our people trained on this. This half day is great, but I'm pretty sure we would need to have short, maybe one-hour refreshers once a quarter to keep it fresh and in front of us."

"That's a good one, Dave," Connie said. "Who else, then?"

Douglas went next. "I like what everyone has said so far. Another thing I want to do is for our bank to use the information internally. I mentioned how I wanted my team to understand how to best communicate with me. I think it would be good if we had the styles for everyone on my team and learned how to better communicate and sell each other. By practicing on ourselves, we would get better with our customers."

There were nods around the table on Douglas's suggestion. "By the way," Douglas added, "I've been trying to adapt a bit by not always going first. I know my high-D can be a bit intense at times. I'll keep working on it. This is new ground for me!" More head nods and smiles followed his comment.

"I guess that leaves me," Connie said. "I've been learning from this workshop at two different levels. First, of course, the buying styles information is invaluable. I think I want to implement some of what all of you said. As Sam has indicated, using it myself will be helpful, in addition to engaging my team to use the information with clients, as Ian and Dave have mentioned, and internally, as you said, Douglas. Outside business, I can see ways to improve how I interact and 'sell' my spouse, as well. I'm looking forward to sharing the information with him.

"I said that I was taking this workshop at two levels. The other thing I've been doing is focusing on the strategies the facilitator used to work with us. This has been the most interactive course I've ever taken. My husband is a professional trainer, and he has shown me a lot about how masterfully facilitators can help people not only learn but completely buy into what they are learning. I'm looking forward to sharing with him some of the techniques used by our facilitator today."

"Can you give us an example of what you are talking about, Connie?" Dave asked.

"I can give you plenty of examples," Connie said. "But you can, too. We have a room full of high-Ds, high-Is, high-Ss, and high-Cs. Think about the various things the facilitator did to keep each style engaged. And it was different for each style. For example . . ."

Just as Connie was about to go into detail, the facilitator told the group, "One minute warning. The clock will sound in 60 seconds."

"That's a good example right there," Dave said. "Who is the clock for? High-Ds, of course." Connie smiled.

"And all the exercises working in teams were for the high-Is, so people would have a chance to speak," Sam pointed out. Connie was nodding.

"And the detailed manual was for the high-Cs," Ian added.

"But what about the high-Ss? What did the facilitator do for them?" asked Douglas.

"I think this was a lot more subtle," Connie said. "First, he kept the discussion warm and friendly—something that is very important to high-Ss. And, even when there were style clashes, the facilitator had us talking about them and in some cases laughing about them.

"But did you notice what he did each time he wanted to get someone involved who was not participating?"

"I did notice that," Sam responded. "I'm usually quiet in groups, and I hate it when people put me on the spot with a question. But, instead of calling on me directly, the facilitator would announce he was going to go around the team and then begin one or two people away from me to give me time to collect my thoughts."

"Exactly," said Connie. "And did it work for you?"

"I guess it did," said Sam, a bit surprised. "It felt . . . considerate."

"Thanks for pointing that out, Connie," Dave said. "We should add to our list that one of the things to implement is to make sure every sales presentation we give to a group has something for all the styles."

··

Detect, Adapt, Beware, Refresh.

··

After having the teams provide their strategies for making different buying styles a part of their sales culture, the facilitator made his final remarks.

"As you leave this workshop and return to your day-to-day work, I want you to focus on four key words: Detect, Adapt, Beware, and Refresh. What do I mean?

- "Be a detective. Actively look for clues that tell you how people want to buy. Your customers have been giving you these clues for years. Now you know how to read them to *detect* their buying styles.

- "Once you understand their buying style, *adapt* your selling style to match. If your customers buy like a high-C, you should sell like a high-C. If they buy like a high-D, sell in that style. When you adapt your selling style, your customers will have the experience they prefer—the experience that helps them buy from you. As Dave said, 'Adapt or continue to be so much less successful than you could be.'

- "*Beware* of the signs that you are selling in the wrong style. If they become impatient, if they are interrupting, if they are actively objecting, if they shut down— these are all signs that you may be selling in the wrong style.

- "Finally, *refresh* your information. You will have forgotten by next week everything you learned today if you don't put in place strategies for using this information on a regular basis. Review it daily or weekly to keep it fresh. Discuss the styles of your customers and prospects with your colleagues. Consciously build your proposals and selling strategies on the basis of what you know about your customers' buying style.

"Detect, Adapt, Beware, and Refresh. These are the keys for long-term success with buying styles. I affirm your success in making buying styles work for you!"

CHAPTER 10

• •

One Year Later

• •

The CEO of CRM First started the meeting. "I've asked Dave, my Vice President of Sales, to join me today to share with you information about the program we have implemented on buying styles."

It was the second Tuesday of the month. Sixteen CEOs had gathered for their monthly meeting as members of Vistage, an organization dedicated to enhancing the personal and professional lives of CEOs, with more than 10,000 members worldwide. This group had been meeting for nearly a decade, and most of the organizations represented had grown between three and five times their size over that time. Two of the organizations had achieved exponential growth and were still growing.

Over the past year, the CEOs had been hearing occasional snippets about CRM First's implementation of buying styles. Though another Vistage member had introduced buying styles to the group, CRM First was the one achieving at high levels. At the preceding meeting, the CEO of the largest company in the group had asked if CRM First would give a 45-minute presentation explaining the concept and what CRM First had done with it.

"Before I turn it over to Dave, I want to compare our performance over the past 12 months with our performance the year before," the CEO from CRM First continued. "Of course, not all the difference can be attributed to implementing a buying styles culture. But we believe the implementation deserves a significant portion of the credit.

"There are a number of statistics I could point to, like revenues being up 25 percent this year, whereas they rose only 11 percent the year before; customer satisfaction numbers at 91 percent this year but only 87 percent the year before; our customer retention numbers at 96 percent this year and 91 percent last year; our sales team turnover at 18 percent this year and 28 percent the year before.

But the most significant number is that our close rate has increased by a third.

"But the most significant number is that our close rate has increased by a third, from 18 percent to 24 percent. Why is this important? Let me explain it this way. Last year, we developed proposals for about $200 million worth of business. Historically, with our normal 18 percent close rate, we would have closed about $36 million of this. But, last year, we closed $48 million. Even if only half of this increase is due to buying styles, it would mean that we did about $6 million more last year in business because of our culture shift. This also means it is costing us less to acquire business because we are more productive with our sales efforts.

"How did we get here? Let me turn it over to Dave to tell you about our journey."

Dave was beaming. It had been an enjoyable year. His team had readily taken to the buying styles approach. Like Connie, Dave had decided to implement all the suggestions that had come from the Red Team that day. Following the meeting, he had met with the CEO to gain approval to hold two half-day sessions at CRM First for all members of the sales department. The first half day covered the information he had learned in the workshop. Three weeks later, during the second half-day session, the sales team used role plays and exercises to practice reading and adapting to the various styles.

Following the training, Dave had volunteers form the company's Buying Styles Team (BST). The BST worked with him on implementing strategies to transform the sales culture.

- The BST came up with the idea of forming ad hoc groups to come together for 15-minute sessions to strategize on the best buying styles approach any time someone was having significant difficulty selling into an account.

- The BST also lobbied and got approval for a special buying style session for spouses so that they could learn the language that would become a part of their loved ones' everyday speech.

- To help with internal communication, the BST created a place on the company's intranet that contained people's self-created extracts from their buying styles personal report, "How to Communicate with Me." In the first month of implementation, the Web page was the most visited space on the company's intranet.

* The BST created voluntary, monthly one-hour refreshers on buying styles over lunch. The BST would bring in lunch for all attendees. Each refresher included a review of buying styles, followed by a focus on a particular client and what had been done to adapt to that company's buying style.

All in all, it had been a very successful undertaking. But, from the workshop, Dave had learned a few other things as well about engaging people.

"I should probably start by giving you an idea of what buying styles are," Dave said to the CEOs. "Think about times when you have been a customer and fill in this sentence for me. I hate it when sales people _____. Think about some of your worst experiences as a customer. Think about the things that salespeople have done that have turned you off. How would you fill in the blank? In your teams, build a list of those sales behaviors that drive you nuts. I am setting the clock to three minutes. . . ."

Afterword

· ·

We hope you have enjoyed *Buying Styles: Simple Lessons for Selling the Way Your Customer Buys.* Our goal was to make the learning adventure an effective way for you to both discover and experience how buying styles can make a difference in every sales interaction.

If you have found the information helpful, make it an integral part of your sales processes. Consider implementing one or more of the strategies that Dave's team found helpful. Detect, Adapt, Beware, and Refresh. And pass the information on to others so that they can benefit as well.

Finally, our highest hope for this work is that the day will come when the approach and language of *Buying Styles* are so widely understood that customers frequently say, "I buy like a high-C, so why don't you sell to me in that style?" and salespeople will know how to deliver the selling experience that customers want.

Here's to success in selling the way your customer buys.

Michael Wilkinson

Richard Smith

Tierah Chorba

Lynn Sokler

We welcome your comments and inquiries about our Buying Styles book, training courses, or other services at Leadership Strategies. Please contact us at 800.824.2850 or see our Web site, www.leadstrat.com.

Appendix: Style Summary

• •

What follows is a summary of each of the four buying styles, including information on how to recognize the style, on selling do's and don'ts, on how to gain their attention, on signs you are selling in the wrong style, and on recommended responses.

High-D Summary
• •

How to Recognize a High-D

Their key factor . . .	Time
They will ask you . . .	What's the bottom line?
If they have a question . . .	They will interrupt and ask
They will tune out if . . .	You take too long to get to the point

How to Sell to a High-D

They want you to:

- Let them control
- Get to the point
- Give them the bottom line

Selling do's:

- Be prepared; tell them what you are going to tell them.
- State your points clearly, briefly, specifically.
- Give only as much detail as necessary; let them be in charge.

Selling don'ts:

- Don't waste their time with idle chatter.
- Don't ramble or tell long stories.
- Don't be too detailed unless they ask for it.

Get their attention:

- *"Suppose I skip the details and just hit the highlights."*

Tailor your approach:

- When presenting, give the recommendation first.
- Be brief in writing; one-page summaries are good; indicate recommendation, the problem it solves, and the benefits to be achieved.
- Don't offer many alternatives; they want your best rec-

ommendation and want to know you have considered the many options for them.

- Stress the benefits of your proposal and how it will bring tangible results.
- Use visual displays, graphs, pictures.

Signs you are selling in the wrong style:

- Impatience, looking at watch, multitasking

How to respond to the signs:

- *"Let me cut to the chase here and give you the bottom line."*

Summary:

> **Be prepared, be brief, be gone.**

High-I Summary

How to Recognize a High-I

Their key factor . . .	Being heard
They will ask you . . .	What's the potential?
If they have a question . . .	They will interrupt and explain
They will tune out if . . .	You focus on facts and figures or don't make it interactive

How to Sell to a High-I

They want you to:

- Give them the stage
- Ask for their ideas
- Keep it fun

Selling do's:

- Give them the big picture before going into details.
- Give them a chance to share their ideas.
- Keep the conversation friendly and warm.

Selling don'ts:

- Don't dwell on details and facts; provide these in writing, instead.
- Don't tell them what to do without giving them an opportunity to respond.
- Don't allow them to ramble too long.

Get their attention:

- *"Let me begin with the big picture."*
- *"What would you say if you could learn of a way to . . .?"*
- *"I have a unique approach for you."*
- *"This is quite innovative—something that really has never been tried before."*
- *"Let me get your thoughts on this approach."*

Tailor your approach:

- Allow ample time; they like expressing, imagining, and discussing.
- Be conceptual; relate to a broader concept or idea.
- Stress uniqueness; they respond to new or out-of-the-ordinary ideas.
- Emphasize future value.
- Start off global and work toward the more specific.

Signs you are selling in the wrong style:

- Interrupting, checking out mentally

How to respond to the signs:

- *"I would like to get your thoughts on . . . brainstorm with me how to . . . let's save the details for later."*

Summary:

Let them sell themselves.

High-S Summary

How to Recognize a High-S

Their key factor . . .   Being liked

They will ask you . . .   Who likes it?

If they have a question . . . They will wait for you to finish

They will tune out if . . .   You become forceful or demanding

How to Sell to a High-S

They want you to:

- Be personable and friendly
- Show an interest
- Make it easy to say yes or no

Selling do's:

- Start with a personal comment.
- Present ideas deliberately and clearly; provide assurances.
- Make sure they are in agreement before moving on.

Selling don'ts:

- Don't dive straight into business.
- Don't be demanding or abrasive.
- Don't assume "silence means consent."

Get their attention:

- *"Let's get acquainted again before we get right down to business."*

- *"Why don't we talk about it over lunch?"*
- *"This will help your people be able to . . ."*
- *"People on your staff will appreciate that Bill Smith, over in _____ company, also thinks this is a good approach."*

Tailor your approach:

- Allow time for connecting with each other.
- Explain the impact of your proposal on others.
- Show how the idea has worked well in the past.
- Indicate how others reacted to ideas, how it meets their needs.
- Maintain good eye contact and personalize conversation.

Signs you are selling in the wrong style:

- Shutting down, becoming passive-aggressive

How to respond to the signs:

- *"There may be good reasons not to do this; let's identify potential strengths and weaknesses."*

Summary:

Start personal; don't assume.

High-C Summary
• •

How to Recognize a High-C

Their key factor . . .   Getting it right

They will ask you . . .   How do you know it works?

If they have a question . . . They will wait to see if you cover it

They will tune out if . . .   You make claims without provid-
                              ing evidence

How to Sell to a High-C

They want you to:

- Provide detailed information
- Provide time for examining
- Provide supporting evidence

Selling do's:

- Present ideas in a logical fashion.
- Stay on topic.
- Provide facts and figures that back up claims.

Selling don'ts:

- Don't be disorganized or make random comments.
- Don't rely on emotional appeal to gain agreement.
- Don't force a rapid decision.

Get their attention:

- *"Let me walk you through this step-by-step."*
- *"I have several approaches for you to look at."*
- *"Before we start, let me bring you up-to-date."*
- *"Let's look at this in a logical, systematic way."*
- *"Why don't you study it and I'll get back with you."*

Tailor your approach:

- Be precise; use ranges and probabilities when precise information is not available.
- Organize your presentation in chronological order or outline it step-by-step.
- Include alternatives, and outline the pros and cons of each.
- Be prepared with supporting data to back up your claims.

Signs you are selling in the wrong style:

- Objecting, arguing, finding fault

How to respond to the signs:

- *"Let's not rush into something unnecessarily . . . let's identify what we know and where we need more information."*

Summary:

> **Give them time for the details.**

Bibliography

Bonnstetter, B. J., & Suiter, J. (2004). *The Universal Language DISC—A Reference Manual.* Scottsdale, AZ: Target Training International.

Jung, C. (1926). *Psychological Types.* New York: Harcourt, Brace.

Kiersey, D., & Bates, M. (1978). *Please Understand Me.* Del Mar, CA: Prometheus Nemesis Books

Lawrence, G. (1982). *People Types and Tiger Stripes.* Gainesville, FL: Center for Applications of Psychological Type.

Marston, W. M. (1928). *The Emotions of Normal People.* UK: Devonshire Press.

Myers, I. B. (1980). *Introduction to Type.* Palo Alto, CA: Consulting Psychologists Press.

Myers, I. B. (1962). *The Myers-Briggs Type Indicator.* Palo Alto, CA: Consulting Psychologists Press.

About the Authors

• •

Michael Wilkinson is CEO of Leadership Strategies—The Facilitation Company (www.leadstrat.com), a national leader in providing organizations with professional facilitators to lead executive retreats, conferences, and task forces. The Atlanta-based company also provides training in facilitation skills, leadership, and sales. For 14 years, Wilkinson served in sales and consulting roles with ADP and with Ernst & Young. His dynamic style makes him a much-sought-after speaker in the United States and abroad. He is the author of two other books: *The Secrets of Facilitation* and *The Secrets to Masterful Meetings*.

Richard Smith is a Principal Facilitator with Leadership Strategies. He has held senior executive positions with responsibility for sales, marketing, services, and support, as well as for all administrative areas. He has led sales teams that have grown revenue from less than $1 million to more than $50 million annually and has established direct sales forces, as well as alternate channels of distribution. He has worked with several sales methodologies, including CustomerCentric Selling,

Solution Selling, SPIN Selling, and the Complex Sale, as well as many CRM products.

Tierah Chorba is CEO of Veritas Visioneering, a catalyst/resource firm that serves organizations seeking to maintain a mission focus while pursuing operational excellence. Formerly a sales and compliance trainer for the nation's largest mortgage training firm and an owner/broker, she leverages her sales insights for her clients by aligning client touch processes with an organization's promise in the marketplace.

Lynn Sokler has more than 30 years of experience consulting to business leaders and government on the best ways to communicate with customers. She has been recognized for her communication work and has won more than 25 national awards. She was named one of the top 50 Healthcare PR Pros in the Nation by *PR Week*. Currently, she is chief of the marketing and communication strategies group at the U.S. Centers for Disease Control and Prevention.